GUILT

THE
SOURCE
& THE
SOLUTION

Guilt

The Source and the Solution

WILLIAM G. JUSTICE

Tyndale House
Publishers, Inc.
Wheaton, Illinois

Library of Congress Catalog
Card Number 81-50294.
ISBN 0-8423-1254-4, paper.

First printing,
September 1981. Printed in the
United States of America.

Dedicated to

Mary F. Justice

my friend
whom I still affectionately call
Mother

CONTENTS

PREFACE

Karl Menninger raised the question, *Whatever Became of Sin?* It was obvious, to those who read the answer to his own question, he was convinced that *sin* is still with us in spite of the unpopularity of the word. Then what of its guilt? While studying the problems related to guilt for more than sixteen years, in preparation for my earlier book, *Guilt and Forgiveness,* (Grand Rapids: Baker, 1981), again and again people raised the question, "Why are you studying the subject of guilt? Nobody feels guilty for anything anymore!" Despite their overstatements, they were partly correct. Such repeated comments demanded some thought. If somebody has "sinned," as Menninger insists, somebody is guilty. But *whatever became of guilt*? Is it truly gone? Or might it be masquerading behind some other name? If so, might it be leaving clues to its identity? If guilt is still among us, why do so many not feel its pain?

Rarely do people use the word "guilt" in normal conversation. Most prefer to say they "feel bad" or they feel "uneasy" about having violated some statute within their moral code. Even when the feeling is really there, they normally choose words that try to hide the feeling of guilt. To oversimplify for the sake of of making a point, guilty people can generally be classified into one of two groups: those who feel virtually overwhelmed by their sense of guilt and those who seem to be unaware of any sense of guilt at all. It is more than a matter of terminology or semantics. Even when someone is severely harmed by their behavior, many people rarely experience the feelings of guilt. Why? Why do so many people feel little or no guilt for their misdeeds?

This book is the result of the search initiated by that question. A student's inquiry during a lecture added impetus to the question: "How many ways do we have to defend ourselves against feeling guilty?" Before the end of the class that day we had listed twelve on the chalkboard.

At the beginning of the following semester, a student from that class received permission from his faculty advisor to do an independent study under my supervision. Donald L. Clark submitted a paper, "Techniques Used to Escape Guilt," in which he added to our original list another twelve ways of defending against the feelings of guilt. Don's paper became the central file to which more than another dozen were added over the next several years. Having read many thousands of pages from published and unpublished works, I remember none (other than Don's) that named more than ten methods commonly used to avoid the feelings of guilt. I suspect that even this compilation is incomplete and I invite additions that may be submitted by those who read these pages.

My purpose here is to produce more than a catalogue. Though we will name and examine the methods commonly used by modern men to escape that pain commonly called a "guilty conscience," we will also examine the damaging, pathological influence of some of them. They can contaminate every dimension of personality. Our coping methods may be more damaging than the sense of guilt we seek to escape. As we look at the damaging methods of handling the sense of guilt, we will also examine the more constructive methods available to us.

This is not an exhaustive study or complete definition of guilt. The literature is full of definitions and you know it by experience. If you did not, you probably would not be reading even these first pages.

Having been a student of human behavior for practically all of my half-century of living, full credit to those responsible is impossible. Somewhere I read: "I am a part of all those after whom I have read, and all those whom I have known." My biggest debt of gratitude is to Donald L. Clark, my former student who first challenged my thoughts in this direction. Chaplains Mark Gaines, Paul Bay, Ed Lester, (my associates) and Bob Klutts (a former associate) have always seemed glad to share as I have "picked their brains." I am grateful also to Joan Milner, an able social worker, psychotherapist, and friend, who pointed out enough weaknesses to require some major revisions. Mrs. Winnie Lamb, a gracious lady of patience, is due a special word of appreciation for her efforts as she typed and retyped materials in the refining process. I also thank Ann, my wife for more than twenty-seven years, for her love, patience, and encouragement.

SOMEBODY'S REALLY GUILTY

The "not I" spirit haunts every home. The top is left off the glue bottle; wet leaves from someone's shoes are on the living room carpet; the front door is left open in the middle of winter. Ask every member of the family and no one admits having made the mistake.

On the construction site, one corner of the concrete foundation of the new apartment building is found to be five inches too high. Ask the fourteen men on the job who was responsible and every one of them can tell you. It was "not I." The experienced job superintendent was almost sure before he asked what the answer would be. This mischievous "not I" spirit is everywhere—in homes, in industry, and in every level of government. If the problem involved only trivialities, we might be able to laugh it off.

But the consequences are serious. There is nothing amusing about the tragedies for which no one accepts the blame. We are sometimes told by renowned scholars that "no one is ever to 'blame.' No one is ever really 'responsible.' "[1] When no one is responsible, the atrocities go on.

We are approaching problems bigger than wet leaves on the living room carpet or a few inches of concrete that can be chiseled away. Such matters are as personal as a man destroying himself with alcohol, as international as a power-hungry government forcibly taking control of its neighbor, and as global as a world poisoning itself with its own waste products.

Who is responsible for the pollution of the once-pure streams of the world? "Not I" says each of those boating off down the lake, strewing trash and garbage in their wake. "My little bit is not enough to count. It's the big industrial plants that are making our waters so filthy."

"Not I," says the industralist. "I'm just providing jobs and putting out a product at the lowest price I can to make a profit for the stockholders and to help keep down inflation. Other means of disposing of industrial wastes would drive up the prices. Besides, everybody else is doing it, and if you want the truth, the real polluters are the large cities who are dumping raw sewage into the streams."

"Not I," says the city mayor. "I am just trying to keep down taxes that would surely have to be raised if we were to build adequate sewage treatment and disposal plants. The culprits are really the individual taxpayers who howl every time we propose some new project." The projected blame has gone full circle with everyone pointing to someone else. They forget to mention the damage by detergents and pesticides for which no one accepts responsibility.

The spirit of "not I" rules, and our lakes and streams have become cesspools and sewage ditches in spite of the best efforts of the few whose cries are heard as echoes in an empty canyon.

And the skies above grow darker. There is nothing humorous about the cartoons we have seen depicting the future when men wear gasmasks while working outdoors. From backyard incinerators, from automobile engines, and from the gigantic industrial smokestacks come the poisons to our sinuses and lungs.

And the earth grows emptier as we deplete its fossil fuels. But we are told not to be concerned. By proper research there will be enough left to supply the world with fuel for another hundred years! The current two or three generations will all have died off by that time and if there are any left behind, let them get along as best they can. Even small children forty years ago were asking how the world could go on recklessly pumping and digging and wasting the natural resources from the earth's depths.

Is no one guilty of wasting the earth's wealth, of putrifying the earth's atmosphere, and of poisoning the earth's waters? And is there no guilt in the uglification of the earth's surface by man-made gorges called strip mines? Is no one guilty as the forests are ravaged of their ancient timbers? Felling the redwoods, some of earth's oldest and tallest trees, men insist, "But it will take us more than thirty years to cut the thousands of acres that haven't been touched yet." But what happens in thirty years when it's all gone? Is there no sin, no immorality in unrestrained waste of resources needed by generations of the future? Is there not true guilt in any behavior that robs or otherwise harms human beings?

Are we not aware of the lives marred every day by the abuse of children? Battered, bruised, and broken, thousands are treated each year in the emergency rooms and pediatric wards of our hospitals. The National Institute of Mental Health reports that each year more than 1.5 million children are attacked by their parents "with enough ferocity to cause injury or death."[2] That fact stirs our concern, as it well ought to do.

But what of the emotional abuse? What of those

children used in the making of pornographic movies in which the children are used to express every conceivable homosexual and heterosexual appetite. Perverted, disturbed, and angered, the odds are high that they will stagger into the world's refuse pits of degenerate souls unless by some miracle they are salvaged. But such human abuse goes on.

Some public schools have had to remove rest room doors and children go to the rest room on the "buddy system" as a precaution against sexual assault by schoolmates of the same sex. The danger is so high and the threat so strong that many children refuse to enter school rest rooms no matter how strong the "call of nature."

We could elaborate on other abuses to persons, such as those within the penal system, where lives are wasted in idleness. A man commits murder and is locked away into stagnant, dependent, uselessness while the dead man's widow, by way of taxation, contributes to the murderer's support. Why should he not be forced to productive labor with the economic returns going to the state or to the dead man's widow and children? Or have we gone so far that such an attempt at justice would be classified as "cruel and unusual punishment?"

We could examine the extent to which mine owners abuse their workers far beneath the earth's surface by skirting governmental regulations and failing to provide adequate ventilation and safety precautions. Or should we examine the extent to which workers cheat their employer by failing to put in an honest day's work for an honest day's pay. Of course, some will always counter that they are not getting an honest day's pay. Everyone has his own defense of his own failings, so that few admit to being guilty of anything.

We could examine the sadistic practices of "knife-happy" surgeons who go on performing unneeded operations while other physicians who know what they are doing look the other way in a conspiracy of silence. Attending nurses shake their heads as though they have heard an unfunny joke with a punch line that said something about "self-policing within the profession."

Maybe those irresponsible physicians would rather that we consider the abuses of the pulpit in which guilt is piled upon guilt as condemnations are poured out upon already burdened people who have come to church looking for relief from their heavy load.

In the event someone has missed the point, let it be said clearly: *actual misdeeds are causing untold misery and harm in this world, and people, individually and collectively, are responsible for it!* We are looking, then, not at guilt feelings, but at *guilt.* People are guilty! Some may or may not *feel* guilty, but for such crimes against man as those just described, human beings are *truly guilty.*

"If it feels good, do it," in some form of paraphrase is the slogan advertisers have pasted on billboards all across our land, in keeping with the mood of the times. A politician sells his influence to redirect a defense contract. A housewife slips off in midafternoon to the bed of a secret lover. A builder hides the installation of inferior materials. An oil tycoon schemes to gouge the powerless consumer. But who feels guilty? Internal adjusting systems are at work.

Someone may charge that these observations are an attempt to pile a heavier load of guilt feeling upon people. I would agree that too many are crushed by guilt feeling already. There is a proper way to deal with these feelings, as we shall see. But rather than cover up guilt, or give it a respectable name, or pretend it doesn't exist, or "psychologize" it away, a healthier alternative for dealing with it is available.

In the meantime, remember that any person who harms himself or another *is actually guilty,* no matter what he does or does not feel, no matter how well he has or has not learned his lessons from experimentation or from the popular press on "How to Do Everything You Want Without Feeling Guilty."[3] Most folks don't need instruction in this anyway.

Some would have us to look the other way and to believe that man is never truly guilty. "There are no norms. There are no standards. There are no universal rights and wrongs. All is relative. All right or wrong is in terms of the particular culture you are observing." By this they imply that we are to live in a world of pretense and ignore the collective and individual sins of man. And some of us tend to welcome such teachings, since they help us "get off the hook." If there really were no sin, there would be no guilt.

But foundational to modern psychology is the teaching that acceptance of reality is essential to good mental health. Can we deceive ourselves into believing that people are not really being harmed by the kind of actions described in the preceding pages? When people are truly harmed, those who are bringing that harm are truly guilty. Again—we are not, at this point, discussing *feeling.* We are looking at actual, real, true guilt.

From all the emphasis this places on behavior, the reader may easily, but erroneously, conclude that I am concerned only with actions. Someone may accurately declare, "You ought to be concerned with attitudes. A man's behavior is largely the outer evidence of what lies within him. It is the heart that rules the head and the head that rules the hands. The seat of the problem lies in greed and envy, in lust and pride, and in the thirst for power and the hunger to avenge." That is all true, but for now let us look at that outer evidence of that which makes men truly guilty.

True guilt *is in that which violates people.* Psychiatrist Karl Menninger would remind the world, "Sin is not against rules, but against people—and it is the 'against-ness' or aggression in the intent or motivation that constitutes the designation of sin."[4] And there is guilt upon those who participate in that which is "against" people—that which harms, demoralizes, takes away from, or tears down the quality of people's lives.

But what of the feelings? The presence of those painful guilt feelings reminds us of our condition. Guilt says, "You are here instead of where you ought to be. You have goofed. You have violated your own accepted standard." And if harm has been done to oneself or to another, guilt says, "You are in touch with reality." The flight from guilt requires denial, fantasy, and at times it may require a degree of insanity. In fact, the degree to which one is in touch with his true guilts may be the degree to which he is truly sane. Or to put it another way, the degree to which one evades his true guilts may be the degree to which he is insane. In the language of Berdyaev, "The sense of guilt liberates us from phantasms and brings us back to real being."[5]

I recently talked with a man who had forsaken his wife and two children. He had left town with a woman who had also forsaken her husband and two children. Now, months later, he is near an emotional collapse. Neither has divorced. He had built up an elaborate enough defense system to be able to carry out his initial actions but when this defense system around his behavior began to crumble, he too began to crumble. His strong sense of guilt was growing out of the fact that persons truly were being harmed. His wife was at home suffering from a broken trust in her husband. His family had been deprived of economic support and his role as a contributing member of a family. Both he and his girl friend were evading all responsibilities to their families. They both had been destroying precious qualities in themselves by their lies and their general life-style together. Since persons were harmed—others *and* themselves—they were miserable in their "true guilt." They were in touch with the reality of their harmful behavior and they were experiencing the tormenting pain of guilt feelings.

The term "true guilts" reminds us that people are often plagued by "false guilts" in that they often feel quite guilty for the violation of points in their ethical code that harm absolutely no one.

Not only do we sometimes want to deny the reality of true guilt, when "guilt feelings" are aroused, we tend to deny them too. That miserable feeling goes by many names, but few dare call it guilt. But look under the cover of the term "Not OKness,"[6] or low self-esteem, or self-hatred, and almost invariably you will find working some ugly old guilt that would prefer to remain concealed. If you want to sound more philosophical, you may call it "existential estrangement" while your studied friend calls it "unauthenticity." Somewhat like the word "sin," the word "guilt" has something of a theological ring that makes people want to deal with it in other terms, if at all. But don't expect to find either the word "sin" or "guilt" very often in contemporary theological writing. A cursory survey of a multi-book collection, *Makers of the Modern Theological Mind*[7] presenting the basic contributions of major theologians of the past 150 years, shows a near-total absence of the words. You may read of men responsible for ethical failures, but not of "sin" and its "guilt." Call it what you will, but to borrow from a worn phrase, "a thorn of any other name is still a thorn," and there is no rose on its stem! It's as though the ideas of sin or guilt were irrelevant to modern life.

Though guilt is a source of pain, it does have its value. When one considers all the pain brought by guilt, it should not seem surprising that anyone would want to escape, but we must not lose sight of the benefits that one may gain from the painful awareness of guilt. It does make a positive contribution to life. It is a pain that urges us to do better.[8] Bear in mind that all pain is not by necessity, destructive. In fact, pain may be the royal but rocky road to growth. In reality, there seems to be little growth among human beings that is not in some way preceded by pain. Pain is not only an invitation to growth; it is usually a prerequisite to it. Pain goads us to "move, change, or do something." As physical pain warns that something is wrong in the body, the pain of guilt is a warning that something is wrong deeper within the self.[9]

A young aviation cadet had an instructor pilot who nagged continuously from the back seat, giving instructions and making corrections. If a serious error were made, he switched off the mike and screamed above the roar of the engine. His voice always came through loud and clear.

On the big day of the first solo flight, it seemed as though he were still in the back seat, naggingly giving instructions, making corrections, and occasionally screaming when something was done wrong.

Every person needs a gently nagging "voice in the back seat." From long ago comes the plea, "labor to keep alive in your breast that little spark of celestial fire, conscience."[10] A mature conscience is one of the most valuable possessions one can have. It can be a healthy goad to constructive behavior. But it is only a goad. It itself is not action.

Some therapists try to use this voice of conscience as a tool to promote healing. Others see different potential values. Both Integrity Therapy and Reality Therapy recognize the value of guilt feelings and the benefit that *can* be derived by one "stewing in his own juice," at least for a while after facing one's true behavior and its consequences to the self or to another. To the person admitting his failing, Integrity Therapy would say, "This suffering of yours is not an indication of weakness; it is a sign of strength. It shows you have some character. If you had no real character structure you wouldn't be worried and upset. Your malaise is a barometer of your value system which will not allow you to continue to live at this low level." Thus Integrity Therapy has a paradoxical emphasis of awareness, of failure and commendation, for the sensitivity which brought on the symptom. Such an attitude is the basis upon which a large part of man's true ego strength is built.[11]

The sense of guilt seems to begin normally somewhere between ages three and six. Some insist that the earliest strains of guilt begin in the love-hate struggle for the parent. Others suggest guilt is a result of the inevitable failure to be able to carry incestuous and murderous fantasies through to fruition. Others would hold that the guilt arises because the child feels he "ought not" have such impulses.[12]

Freud said that feelings of guilt stem from the fear of loss of love. Adler was sure it came from the refusal to accept one's inferiority, and Jung was equally convinced that guilt-feelings stem from man's refusal to accept himself wholly, failing to integrate his "shadow self" into consciousness.[13] We'll leave such discussion to the developers of theory and move on to that which is more in keeping with more familiar struggles nearer where we live day by day.

Because the sense of guilt is a kind of pain and inner strife, it is commonly seen as an enemy; not an invading enemy, but an enemy within; a traitorous enemy of self; an enemy to battle, and to defend the self against; an enemy that can inflict pain, incapacitate, do bodily harm, destroy peace of mind, and can even kill. But somewhat in the fashion of the Perry Mason mystery novel, the truth is revealed that guilt feeling is not the culprit.

The real enemy to peace within is the misbehaving self.

Guilt arrives on the scene instantly following the "crime." Guilt feelings arrive after an inner courtroom trial. We are not merely playing with words. We are looking at the distinction between guilt and guilt feelings. Guilt is that which one takes on at the initiation of that act or attitude which brings harm to another or to one's self. *People are guilty.* They may or may not *feel* guilty. The guilt feeling is the warning signal that something is wrong. Again borrowing from Menninger's definition, guilt may be defined as the results of one willfully offending or harming *anyone.* It is the results of the "willful disregard or sacrifice of the welfare of others for the welfare or satisfaction of the self."[14]

But when we consider that man somewhat steps outside himself and relates to himself, we realize that man often works against his own best interests, "sinning" against himself. He is often guilty of harming himself far more than he would ever harm another. He is still guilty! One is guilty any time he serves that which stifles, cuts down, depletes, erodes, narrows, or depreciates life—his own or that of another.[15] Whether on the surface or hidden from awareness, a prolonged sense of guilt becomes destructive.

For more than three decades, knowledgeable medical

people have been telling us that our inner conflicts can and do make us physically ill, creating psychogenic disorders. When the writers in the field of psychosomatic medicine established their theories, they were often ridiculed and challenged. "Give us clinical proof that inner stresses can or do help produce illnesses. Give us more than mere idle observations that 50 to 80 percent of the patients in general hospitals today are there for diseases triggered by internal conflicts." Researchers accepted the invitation and the results are available for the world to read in the layman's nontechnical language.[16] In *Type A Behavior and Your Heart,* Doctors Friedman and Rosenman make it quite clear that an "error in spirit" leads to catastrophic "failure in matter."[17] We know that 48 to 52 percent of the deaths in the United States in recent years have been attributed to heart disease. We know also that the stress of living outside one's value system is a major contributor to some of the most common forms of heart disease. Therefore, the problem of guilt is worthy of serious consideration even if it were associated only with heart disease. But we know that such stress is also responsible, or a major contributing factor, to more than one hundred other physical illnesses!

If we look at the cost only in terms of physical illness, that would be serious enough, but that is only a beginning. The toll is even higher in forms of mental anguish. The psychotherapist sees so much pain from guilt that he tends to breathe a sigh of despair on behalf of those he serves. Unfortunately, all too often, the therapist is just as lost as his patient in dealing with the problem of guilt. In an effort to relieve the burden, the therapist may work endlessly to persuade the client not to feel responsible for his misery. The culprits, he is told, are his parents and the society in which he lives. Such therapists support their client's defense systems against guilt. At best, this answer only postpones the painful guilt feelings. His client is harmed instead of healed.

We live under the discerning judgment of our fellow creatures. We also live under the scrutiny of our inner judge. Guilt feeling is a price paid by the self upon hearing the inner tribunal pronounce its judgment of "Guilty." How guilty or how lacking in guilt one *feels,* depends almost entirely upon the effectiveness of his inner "trial court" defense system.

For every failure to do, to act, to think, to feel, or to be as we feel we "ought," an inner voice of conscience rises to accuse. In "the courtroom of the mind," where men try and condemn themselves, each person plays the role of all the separate courtroom personalities for every violation of his sense of "ought." We are our own judge and jury; our own accuser and defender; our own witness and recorder of the process. Having violated our own code of behavior, we stand as a criminal on trial. The conscience then goes on to try, to convict, to condemn, to damn, to torment, and it may even call for an execution. The trial may last no more than a moment, but the execution may be carried out through installment payments over the span of many years.

A value judgment has been made in the foregoing pages when I have said that we are truly guilty when we have harmed any person. We must examine even more fundamental criteria for that judgment and for any of man's judgment of himself.

CRITERIA FOR DETERMINING TRUE GUILT

The basis for judging our own behavior and that of others comes from sources too numerous to count and often too subtle to name. Parents, siblings, friends, teachers, religion, nationalism, superstitions, our own experience, and the general culture all contribute their bit. Everyone seems to want to write into our code book what we ought and ought not do. We make laws for ourselves by which we make judgment of our actions, thoughts, attitudes, and feelings. We usually classify them into categories of "good and bad," "right and wrong," or "moral and immoral." When we or others judge something about us as good, right, or moral, we are likely to turn on some pleasant, warm, enjoyable feeling within ourselves. But when that judgment is bad, wrong, or immoral, we are likely to experience an unpleasant feeling from which we want desperately to escape or against which we feel compelled to defend ourselves.

TOTAL ESCAPE

Let us suppose for a moment that the internal escape or defense system against guilt feeling has become totally perfected. The person has been able to think, or speak, or act in any conceivable way without ever having the slightest trace of guilt feeling. He has either killed such feelings or has learned to conceal them from himself. Such persons seem to exist, and psychiatrists label them as sociopathic or psychopathic personalities.

Some might want to believe that such a person had attained paradise, and many would envy them. The naive believe that such a person is truly carefree and contented. This isn't necessarily true because he quickly meets hostile barriers. A person who does or says that which invariably satisfies only himself intrudes into the rights of others. When one is unfeeling and unaware of his own true guilt, people around him are made to suffer.

BUT CONSEQUENCES BEGIN

Though a man may fail to live within his own ethical code or he may even refuse to form one, others will form one for him and demand that he live by it. A country store philosopher said it well. "Your rights end where my nose begins." Others form rules and we will live by them if we are to remain with them in peace.

Such rules, for instance, may be "You may not steal my purse nor may you intentionally harm someone I love. You may expect consequences if you violate either of these laws that I passed long before you and I met. My law says you have limits. My law says you may not steal from me or harm someone I love no matter what you feel about it." A few days ago I heard a pointed discussion: "You are trying to infringe on my rights by asking that I not smoke when we are in a meeting together." The response came, "Your rights end where mine begin. I have the right to breathe clean air. You are free to smoke all you want unless it invades the air

I must breathe. Your smoke rapes my lungs. I won't tolerate that!" The idea was clear. "If you violate my laws you can expect to suffer the consequences."

Nature has laws that we will not violate without suffering the consequences. We may not be able to quote the physical laws of heat transfer, nor the laws of gravity, but we know that we cannot stick our hands in the fire nor leap from the top of a ten-story building without suffering consequences. And these laws did not suddenly go into effect the day that some scientist was finally able to get them into words.

It seems that no one has yet put into words the "laws of tobacco and industrial pollution," but a visit to any general hospital or conversation with any lung specialist will produce ample testimony that tobacco smoke and industrial pollution have consequences to the respiratory system of smokers and nonsmokers. We say the respiratory system pays the consequences.

Neither the wording of these laws nor the knowledge of the existence of these laws change the consequences. Just as the small child who sticks bobby pins into the electrical outlet suffers the consequences of his behavior, others suffer the consequences of breathing pollutants.

Though we have used the word behavior in relation to the child sticking hair pins into the electrical outlet, we might have more accurately referred to his misbehavior. We use the word misbehavior to identify actions harmful either to the self or to someone else. Whether someone has referred to the behavior as wrong or not makes little or no difference.

A BASIS FOR RIGHT AND WRONG

We would do well to think of wrong (and right) on the basis of the consequences rather than on the basis of opinion. We might then possibly get a glimpse of the basis of all right and wrong.

Every ethical value seems to be based on one major principle: if a behavior harms someone, diminishes him, degrades him, or takes from his life, the behavior is classified as wrong or bad (guilty). If, on the other hand, the behavior uplifts, strengthens, encourages, or works toward life or a higher quality of life, the behavior or attitude is called right or good (unguilty). Erich Fromm called this the basic philosophy of "Bioethics."

Good is all that serves life; evil is all that serves death. Good is reverence for life, all that enhances life, growth unfolding. Evil is all that stifles life, narrows it down, cuts it into pieces. . . . The conscience of the biophilous person is not one of forcing oneself to refrain from evil and to do good. It is not the superego described by Freud, which is a strict taskmaster, employing sadism against oneself for the sake of virtue. The biophilous conscience is motivated by its attraction to life and to joy; the moral effort consists in strengthening the life-loving side in oneself. For this reason the biophil does not dwell in remorse and guilt which are, after all, only aspects of self-loathing and sadness. He turns quickly to life and attempts to do good.[1]

It appears to me that the ethical teachings that grow out of all the world's great religions may have at their foundation the basic principle of this philosophy that says, "good serves life and evil serves death to the personality." Each culture seems to use this principle as it builds its code of ethics, based upon its understanding of what contributes to life and death. Are we then looking upon the foundation of some universal value etched into the very heart of mankind that transcends culture? I think we are. If so, then we should be able to point to some universal rights and wrongs. If that which contributes to life is basically good and that which contributes to death is basically evil, then the most basic evil would be the killing of a human being—not necessarily the physical death, but the murder of the personality—any personality; one's own or another's.

Even if we were considering only the taking of physical life, the principle would still apply. Someone will quickly object, "But there are groups, even whole cultures that not only kill freely but take pride in doing so." But can you imagine a culture that tolerates killing just anyone, even one's own tribesman, just because he has the urge to kill?

But we are looking at more than the taking of physical life. We are looking at that which destroys the very soul—the personality—the character—the humanness of the human being.[2] We are talking of that which contributes to the decay, the coarsening of the spirit, the rot of the heart[3] (greed, envy, hatred, infidelity, etc.). We are looking at that which is pro-death over against that which is pro-life. It is upon this pro-life pro-death principle that all true values are built. Laws of fairness, laws of loyalty, and laws of rights all have behind them a universal value—a value held by mankind. Consider the words of the respected philosopher, C. S. Lewis:

I know that some people say the idea of a Law of Nature or decent behavior known to all men is unsound, because different civilizations and different ages have had quite different moralities. But this is not true. There have been differences between moralities, but these have never amounted to anything like total differences. If anyone will take the trouble to compare the moral teachings of say, the ancient

Egyptians, Babylonians, Hindus, Chinese, Greeks and Romans, what will really strike him will be how very like they are to each other and to our own. . . . Think what a totally different morality would mean. Think of a country where people were admired for running away in battle, or where a man felt proud of double-crossing all the people who had been kindest to him. . . . Men have differed as regards to what people you ought to be unselfish to . . . but . . . selfishness has never been admired.[4]

If there is such a thing as a universal value, it would, indeed, seem to be based on this pro-life principle. That which pulls man away from death, building upward, inclining toward life, we call good. And that which diminishes life, pulling toward death is that which is classified as bad.

From where does such a basic value written into the very fabric of mankind originate? That question makes little more sense than the question that asks, "From where does the capacity for reason originate?" Though we cannot answer these questions with certainty that satisfies all minds, we do know that both man's capacity for reasoning and his capacity for moral judgments are possible because of the part of the brain called the neocortex. Many insist that it is this unique possession, differentiating him from all other animals, this portion of the brain, that most uniquely makes man what he is—man. It is there in the neocortex that he makes moral decisions. There he evaluates attitudes and actions before and after the fact. There he experiences satisfaction with himself or feels guilt. There resides his inclination toward life or toward death; toward good or toward evil; toward that which is constructive or erosive of personality.

THE LAW OF MORTIGRESSION

Notice three phenomena of nature. First, consider an eroding hillside. With each rain soil is washed away. With each freeze the surface is expanded, loosened, and made more vulnerable to the rains and winds that follow. The process is typically slow and generally unnoticeable until the larger scars one day are obvious. Those who have flown over southern Oklahoma have seen this kind of erosion in its extreme form. The Grand Canyon is an even more obvious illustration.

Next consider the boulder rolling down a hill. The farther it goes, the faster it goes, and the more difficult it is to stop.

While these two phenomena of nature are set aside momentarily from thought, consider a basic law of physics. The law of momentum is stated approximately: "A body at rest tends to remain at rest, and a body in motion tends to remain in motion unless acted upon by an outside force."

Now consider these three facts of nature together. That which erodes, detracts, diminishes, or takes away from life may be compared to the rain or wind, eroding, taking away from our hillside, making it less and less than it was before. It disintegrates and washes away with nothing to stop the process, somewhat like the boulder rolling down the hill. In reality, the tiny particles of soil are but miniature boulders. A man who lives in the edge of the Great Smoky Mountain National Park told of having been in the mountains fishing when a sudden summer cloudburst dumped its rain upon the mountains above. Hearing a thunderous noise, he fled the stream to higher ground, barely escaping the avalanche of water and boulders, some as big as automobiles, rolling, bouncing down the mountainside as mere pebbles.

Calling upon the law of momentum, we are reminded that the particles of soil, or boulders, as the case may be, will continue down the hillside unless acted upon by an outside force. But it is *not* the ongoing movement of the soil or boulders that we are primarily concerned with at this moment but the *erosive process.* The actual erosion itself will continue on and on unless acted upon by some outside force. Drawing on all these parallels in nature, we might recognize that *a personality in the process of disintegration* (erosion) *will continue in the process of disintegration unless acted upon by an outside force.* This I call the "Law of Mortigression."

DISINTEGRATION IN PROCESS

The student of Latin will immediately recognize the literal translation of this word "mortigression" as the law of "movement toward death." Ernest Ligon says:

Integration is a condition of personality in which all of the emotional attitudes are harmonious and mutually helpful, thus permitting all of one's natural energy to be directed toward one end. Thus, integrated action is coordinated action in an organism or machine.[5]

Disintegration, therefore, is a condition in which inner attitudes are uncoordinated and at odds. They are in conflict as inner opposing forces.

That which makes the human personality function as a unity begins to work somewhat as gears in a machine that fail to mesh. It is not only disfunctional, but if the inner forces are strong enough, it begins to come apart. Slang expressions of the 1970s referred to a person "falling apart" or becoming "unglued." Such common expressions recognize man's potential for movement away from life toward death. Attitudes and resultant behavior that help in the disintegrative process are called evil or wrong because they are self-defeating, working toward the death of the self and often toward the death of another.

The pro-death, erosive, disintegrative process is almost unnoticeable. Who notices one pebble missing from a hillside? Who notices one crumb missing from half a pie? If one crumb at a time is removed over a long period, we are not likely to pay any attention. And the human personality may be vaguely compared to a pie, at least for the purpose of understanding an important point. The first bite into the whole is the part most noticeably missed. It is the flaw in the perfect. But after a few bites are gone, one more or less is not especially noticeable. Though it is being eaten away, it might be said to be disintegrating. Of course, we are not concerned with a pie but with the tragedy of the disintegrating personality—a psychic fragmentation.[6]

As the disintegration goes on, the personality becomes weaker. Inhibitions are weakened. The power of resistance is lowered. The inner strength of personality is diminished. Character is depleted. The damaging behavior is easier to repeat. And we must reaffirm that each repetition further erodes or eats away at the personality. The pie diagram, used largely for the ease of graphic illustration, is a fairly accurate comparison. It is like the cancer that slowly overcomes and destroys the healthy tissue.

AN INNER JUDGMENT

But deep within, a tiny voice seems to say, sometimes in a whisper, sometimes in a scream, "Don't do that to yourself." Something within judges the way we treat ourselves and others. It says, "You are guilty." It seems to have the wisdom to know that we are damaging ourselves. This wisdom seems more evident when we occasionally see it within the child who is sometimes "wiser than his years." The student of Transactional Analysis would call this interesting facet of the child's self, the "Little Professor." I suspect this same "Little Professor" grows up but gets lost from sight. How do we distinguish between a facet of the self that is "naturally wise" and that facet of the self that has *acquired* wisdom? Call it what we wish. One thing is certain. Something within seems to scream, "How dare you take on attitudes and behaviors that tend to erode the personality!" We each live with an inner judge, who demands payment for every violation of that which we know to be destructive.

We experience pain in both the anticipation of payment and in the payment itself. For the verdict of guilty, we may be forfeiting self-esteem and the sense of self-worth. We tend to feel worth-less after each conviction, paying from whatever reserve we may have of our sense of worth.

WE WANT TO ESCAPE THE PAIN OF JUDGMENT

The loss of self-worth initiates an experience of grief for having forfeited something that was precious and valuable to our sense of well-being. How do we escape that most persistent enemy of inner peace? How do we still that inner voice of accusation that demands some form of payment in the form of suffering? How do we turn off that vivid, detailed, mental record of failure to do or be what we felt we "ought"? How do we cope with the haunting, painful, inner sense of failure that tends to return to be relived again and again? How do we live with the sense of shame and anxiety that we call the "guilty conscience"? The mind will take only a limited amount of pain before it tries to devise some method of relief. It needs help to endure such an insult to the ego.[7]

WE CALL UPON MECHANISMS OF DEFENSE

The chosen method for coping with any emotional pain is commonly referred to as a *coping device* or an *adjusting mechanism.* The personality requires some adjusting means of returning to at least some degree of quietude. Since many feelings are experienced as an attack upon the sense of well-being, we refer to the coping methods as *mechanisms of defense.* Of course, we are using commonly used psychological terms. Here we are looking specifically at the defense against the feelings of guilt.

Many people appear to have so adjusted themselves to their feelings of guilt that they rarely admit to feeling guilty for anything. But the load of guilt is often hidden behind a veil of symptomatic behavior. One may act out a sense of guilt in a type of charade. Those in the therapy professions observe that one's pattern of behavior may be a clue to his underlying struggle with hidden guilt.

Keep in mind that the behaviors to which we will sometimes point are intended to be used as clues to guilt and not as conclusive evidence. Just as a headache may be a clue to anything of severity from minor tension to a brain tumor, behavior that we will discuss may point to virtually nothing at all. Or it may point to cancer-like guilt, gnawing, eroding, deteriorating, degenerating, and debilitating, steadily destroying the whole personality. Many students of personality are convinced that "of the many psychological reactions . . ., guilt is potentially the most dangerous and destructive."[8]

We will, therefore, study both; patterns of thinking

and patterns of misbehavior characteristic in man's struggle to escape the pain of a guilty conscience. It should not be considered unusual that anyone would choose to diminish the pain of guilt. We have chosen means of coping with almost all pain.

If we have a tack in our shoe, we have several options. We may limp along and endure it, hoping that after a while it will go away. Or we may hope that a callus will form and grow tough enough to keep it from hurting so much, or we can "psyche" ourselves into believing it doesn't exist and that it doesn't really hurt. That can be done. We may bend the tack over with a hammer. Or we may go buy new shoes. But we are going to do something about it even if it is only passive endurance of the distress.

Pain of guilt can be worse. And it too calls for some response or combination of responses with quite a large number of options available. While it may be obvious that many of the chosen options for coping with the pain of guilt somewhat overlap, each one may be used separately or several may be employed at the same time. For instance, denial may be the sole mechanism of defense against the painful feelings of guilt or it may be used along with opiates or with what we call scapegoating. At the same time, denial seems to be a part of almost all the mechanisms of adjustment to the complex feelings of guilt. Each mechanism of defense is different enough from the others to justify separate discussion.

A general study of man's defense mechanisms is beyond the intended scope of this book. We are to consider the mechanisms of defense used to adjust to the *painful feelings of guilt!* The same defense mechanisms may be pulled into service to defend oneself against loneliness, sorrow, fear, or any number of other potential threats to the sense of well-being.

Nor am I intending to suggest that all defense mechanisms are necessarily bad or harmful. Indeed, they may sometimes help us function and to maintain our sanity. We arc only trying to better find out what ever became of guilt.

OFFENSIVE DEFENSE AGAINST GUILT FEELINGS

The words strife, conflict, defense, and struggle are common words used to refer to warfare. Opposing forces, holding conflicting ideologies form an alliance for strength in battle and for mutual defense. Each side always justifies its position and justifies the use of its particular tools of war. In each soldier's mind, he is on the side of right, and the higher the values for which he fights, the more vicious the fight and the more deadly the battle.

There is probably no field of battle with a more serious contention than those battles which go on within the human breast. We use the same vocabulary to describe the warring factions within the individual that we commonly use to refer to any other war. The words strife, struggle, conflict, and stress can all point to a fight within. Most of us know the war between right and wrong.

When right prevails, there is at least a temporary peace, but he is in error who would speak of peace only as the absence of war. There is peace only when there is harmony. An active war may have ceased with no semblance of peace. In most instances, when the fighting has stopped, only then do the opposing forces begin to work together to build a harmonious relationship that may, at a later time, be called peace. What the world has often called peace has been only a lull between battles, a lull used to regroup forces for a war more fierce than the previous.

When wrong wins in the battle for the influence on behavior, there is virtually no lull at all. An even more terrible battle is in the making as new warring factions rise to contend. Those forces one has integrated within himself seem to mobilize into an underground army designed for rebellion. "Down with the ruling forces and punish the leader," becomes the battle cry of that warring faction we call the guilty conscience. Here is created a no-man's-land known by many of us.

Most of us have either personally witnessed the terrible ravages of war or we have at least seen the evidences of the destruction on our television screens or on the pages of our newspapers. Since the suffering and waste of human life is to be avoided in any way possible, the commander plans his strategy with design to reduce the enemy but with the least cost to himself and his own forces.

A worn adage says that the best defense is a good offense. To defend an army against the anticipated enemy attack, a surprise attack may be launched before the enemy can pull together his forces.

Since the feelings of guilt come as an attack upon the inner sense of well-being, almost always inflicting pain, we feel it necessary to defend ourselves. In the battle with the guilty conscience, we can launch a rather effective offensive defense, but the tactics are relatively few in number.

REPETITION

Repetition is a tactic with a callousing effect. A man who has done little physical labor may pick up his tools on the first warm day of spring and prepare the soil to plant a garden. By the end of the day his hands may be blistered or raw. But if he works at it every day for the entire summer, his hands will become tough and calloused. A guilt-producing behavior can have much the same effect. If the behavior is repeated again and again, the emotional discomfort is lost as the conscious emotional reponse is deadened to the calloused conscience.

The callousing effect may be either intentional or unintentional. That is, one may consciously decide, "This behavior makes me feel guilty. If I repeat it again and again, I can reduce these feelings and will eventually be able to perform this kind of behavior without feeling any guilt at all." And he *can* do it! It is so effective it is prescribed by occult Satan worship.[1]

But damage is still being accomplished. He is still violating the earlier formed ethical code and his guilt is hidden only from conscious awareness. The erosion goes on. The damage to the self and others goes on.

BALANCING

Balancing the scales or overbalancing the scales, otherwise known as compensation, has been called "a fighting attempt to save the ego."[2] It is the exaggeration of a desirable trait to reduce feelings of failure for not being the person one feels he ought to be, or for not doing as one feels he ought to do. The act of compensation tends to draw attention away from the defect in behavior. It tries to tip the scales to make the good outweigh the bad. We know that we may be far more threatened by self-condemnation than by the condemnation of others. The purpose of the compensating is, therefore, the aggressive attempt to preserve the endangered self.

The philandering husband may try to preserve his sense of integrity by being overly affectionate to his wife and children. "With my good behavior I can make up (compensate) for the bad." "See how much I love them" distracts his attention from admitting, "See how little I love them and express it by betraying their confidence in me."

We must admit that some good is often accomplished in the efforts to compensate, but since one rarely feels quite caught up, the scales always seem tipped in the direction of the bad. He has done wrong and therefore must do much more good in his effort to balance out what he has done bad. Deep inside, however, his judge keeps convicting him of fresh crimes that need to be balanced. Not having yet caught up on balancing out that for which he was already convicted, he must now try harder. Day by day the task of balancing the bad with the good becomes more and more impossible. He must, therefore, blend in additional tactics for dealing with the distressed conscience.

CONFESSION

Confession generally is seen as a highly assertive and healthy way of dealing with our guilts. But contrary to popular thought among the religious and irreligious, confession, in and of itself, is not necessarily beneficial. There is nothing automatically constructive in the act whether it be to a friend, a gospel minister, a priest, or to a secular priest—a psychiatrist.

It is not uncommon for one to decide, "I will admit my faults and will thereby purge myself of my sense of guilt." All would do well to heed the words of a Roman Catholic writer, Caryll Houselander:

Confession and self-accusation, used to escape from the suffering of the feeling of guilt, disintegrate and destroy personality. When it is habitual as with those who confess all their moral lapses to their friends, it has the effect of weakening the will more and more, until ultimately the whole character crumbles.[3]

She warns of the practice of continually confessing moral lapses to friends that is

. . . always punctuated by exaggerated expressions of self-disgust, and go together with a complete absence of any determination to take practical steps to break off the habits in question. Just below the surface of deliberate thought, the person indulging in these confessions reasons thus: "I am not just an ordinary sensualist; if I were, I should not suffer like this for my peccadilloes. Only a sensitive person like myself could suffer such distress for these things." Thus he restores his self-esteem by creating an imaginary, sensitive self who, once more, is "not as other men," and at the same time he is paving the way for future lapses.[4]

Houselander has said it clearly. Confession expressed only for the purpose of relieving the pain of the guilty conscience has highly destructive potential! Why? There are several additional reasons beyond these already given.

First, open confession makes rationalization easier. "Here is what I did, but here is why I did it." Then instead of admitting reality, what appears to be a surrender is manipulated into an intellectual mode of escape. This rationalization, blended with the cathartic "getting it off the chest" produces a bittersweet "guilt cocktail" and a resultant temporary "high." The stage thus is set for the most destructive of guilt's force; the compulsion to self-atonement.

Healthy confession must be the initiation of a process. When confession is uncomplicated by repentance (change) or restitution, the high lets down and one finds himself in further self-castigation, which as we shall see in a later chapter, leads to further moral lapse.

Also, confession only as a relief from guilt feelings often induces a false sense of humility, so strong that one may actually feel proud of his humility. "I'm really a great fellow to be so humble. See how great I am to admit my faults. Anyone as great as I really doesn't need to change."

The positive dimension of confession will be mentioned later.

In addition to the precautions already given is the reminder that confession may be only another symptom of a disease rather than an effective method of relief. Because of the pain in self-humiliation, self-abasement, and renunciation, confession may be added as an implement of self-torture. " . . . the retention of guilt for its pain and the compulsion to confess for its humiliation, may be ways one devises to administer the punishment his low self-image demands."[5]

When direct frontal attack fails to adequately protect from the pain of guilt we must look for some other possible ways of living with it.

SURRENDER TO GUILT FEELINGS

When an army or an individual soldier can no longer fight an effective battle and is in danger of total destruction, surrender may be the only reasonable option. Self-preservation may be the only motive, but at least two additional motives may be present.

Surrender may be made in order to build a true peace, but it may be only a drastic tactical maneuver. It is made with the attitude, "I surrender for now in order to survive. You think the war is over. I am only temporarily defeated. I have lost the battle, but I may still win the war." But the primary purpose for surrender is survival.

Men normally give up in the face of devastation. It has happened again and again on the blood-soaked plains of the world and it has happened again and again in the guilt-soaked canyons of the mind. The spirit, in danger of being crushed in the conflict with guilt, may wave the white flag of surrender: "I won't try to hold my position any longer. I won't fight it anymore."

THAT'S JUST THE WAY I AM

"That's just the way I am," is a favorite form of "give-up-itis." There is no denial of the behavior that has brought harm to the self or to another, but it is a denial of responsibility. "I'm not responsible. I'm just naturally irresponsible." When a load of guilt becomes almost unbearable, we tend to lose hope and throw up our hands in despair: "What's the use? I can't help it. I know I really ought not act as I did, but that's just the way I'm made. I'm so weak I can't resist my temptations."

With such an attitude it is easy to fall back on fate in any of its forms. If one is inclined toward astrology he may affirm, straight-faced, and without apology, that since he was born under a certain sign, he can do no other than he does. It is written in the stars that he must behave in a given way.

It is just as easy to use the fatalistic attitude and relate it to a concept of God. "I'm just the way God made me. If God hadn't wanted me to do as I do, he would have made me in such a way that I wouldn't even want to do it." "What is to be will be."

Another may say, "I have to be as I am because of the way I was treated as a child." Another may add, "That's just human nature."[1] Feelings of guilt are reduced and people continue to be injured.

PASSAGE OF TIME

The passage of time is an apparent friend of the guilty. It does not really erase the guilt but it does have a way of numbing the pain. This seems possible because of the dulling of the memory and because one learns to live with it, in the same manner one may learn to live with an arthritic shoulder. The pain may be always there but after several years he notices it with less frequency.

Also, like the arthritic shoulder, it still may sometimes cost him sleep. It is there, always draining from his effectiveness.

SELF-RECRIMINATIONS

Self-recriminations invite pity and reassurance. They want and expect to hear, "Come now, you really aren't so bad. Look at all of your good qualities." Thus, the outside person's reassurances provide a boost to the sense of self-respect. As Karen Horney points out, such a person hears implied that "he has such a keen moral judgment that he reproaches himself for faults which others overlook and thus ultimately they make him feel that he is really a wonderful person."[2] A bonus value in self-recrimination is in the diversionary benefit. He can easily cloud any issue of true weakness to his own eye or to that of another.

EVERYBODY'S DOING IT

Everybody's doing it is a form of rationalization. Simply because the behavior is a common practice there seems to be a reduction of the sense of guilt by a form of dilution. In June 1970 the Chicago *Sun-Times* wrote that lie detector samplings revealed startling results. It showed that 72 percent of the department store employees, 86 percent of the truck drivers, and 82 percent of the bank employees who were tested were involved in the "fringe benefits" of theft.[3] A man tells himself that he is just doing as others are doing and that his behavior is no worse than the behavior of others around him.[4]

"No worse" is easily translated into "better." One thus emerges with the temporary feeling of being relatively clean. Further self-deception makes it easy to translate relatively clean into clean. The defendant before the inner court then walks away with little conscious awareness of any sense of wrong-doing.

But with the smallest crack in the wall of defense against the pain of guilt, the self begins to agree with Mahatma Gandhi, "In matters of conscience, the law of the majority has no place."[5]

With even the most elaborate system of rationalization, most people soon learn that a simple surrender to their impulses is an intolerable state. Such weakness only depletes the self-image and esteem, adding to the pain. More effective means must be sought.

ESCAPE FROM GUILT FEELINGS

Those who flew combat aircraft with the Strategic Air Command during the days of the Korean War became intimately acquainted with the techniques of escape, evasion, and survival taught by the U.S. Air Force. Flight personnel were taught specific measures to employ in the event of capture by the enemy. They were taught evasive tactics for eluding the enemy and how to survive in enemy territory while working their way back toward friendly land.

After many hours of classroom work led by highly skilled and experienced instructors, the crewmen were placed in the field for practical maneuvers in simulated enemy territory and hunted by their instructors who took the role of enemy. The consequences of being captured were so severe that hundreds of mothers complained to their senators and congressmen who responded with congressional investigations. What were their conclusions? "Yes, your sons are being treated harshly. But they are being trained to come out of enemy territory alive!" Of course, not all came out alive, but many of those who did survive did so because they had learned their escape, evasion, and survival tactics, and learned them well.

As we have considered already, the guilty conscience is commonly experienced as an enemy. And we sense that it can be a deadly one. The one purpose of the guilty person may be to stay alive. There is no simulated action, and there are no war games. We learn the survival tactics in the combat zones of life, and if we feel compelled to surrender, we know we may be tormented and left to rot in our own moral dungeons.

Those airmen were taught, "If you are captured, your consuming purpose becomes, to stay alive and to escape!" Instructors were no ivory-towered theorists. They were those who had themselves escaped from prisoner-of-war camps. "Escape! Escape! Your purpose is to get away from your torturous captors and to get back to friendly lines." Many of those who were shot down over enemy terrain were taken captive even before their parachutes fully collapsed around them.

Would they be killed? Would they be tortured? Would they die in some vermin-infested POW camp ten thousand miles from home? We know the answer was yes for too many of them. Some were killed outright and others were tortured. Bamboo shafts were jammed beneath the fingernails. Fingers were chopped off bits at a time. Electrical shock was applied to the gonads.

We tend to cringe in face of the very thoughts of such torture. But the guilty conscience can torture also. As one immediately recoils from the distressful shock of an electrical impulse, there is a recoil from the distress of the pain inflicted by the guilty conscience. The problem continues, "How do I escape? How do I turn it off? How do I get away from the torment? How can I keep from feeling guilty? It hurts!" When a previously used method fails, we look for another. We experiment. Then we usually settle on those methods that seem to work best for us.

When irresponsibility and surrender are no longer tenable and bring additional loss of self-respect, we almost instinctively turn to escapist patterns of thought or behavior.

SUPPRESSION

By suppression of a guilt-producing experience, one says, "I can't bear to look." He consciously tries to keep the memory of the experience out of his thoughts. He is working to block any recall from the conscious memory. There is no clear line of demarcation between suppression and repression except that repressed material has been pushed to a level of unconsciousness. Suppression can be compared to holding a tennis ball under water. Just one or two may present little problem, but try it with a dozen and you will have yourself a full-time job. Suppression is a conscious effort to forget; to push the experience and its associated feelings from the mind. In suppression one says, "If I can keep from thinking about it, I'm all right, I'm comfortable."

But like the tennis balls, they keep bobbing back to the surface. By the time one is pushed under others are popping up. The analogy may seem vaguely amusing but since guilt produces pain each time it surfaces, there is nothing funny about it. If you pictured the analogy in your mind you see a fellow quite busy at work. It can be a full-time job.

Since it requires large expenditures of psychic energy, we should not be surprised that one who is working to suppress his guilt often complains, "I feel tired all the time." Or, "I sleep all night but wake up just as tired as I was when I went to bed." Expenditures of emotional energy drain physical energy. Thus, one who is suppressing much may really be tired all the time. One of the most common complaints heard by physicians is related to the feeling of being chronically fatigued. The patient may go from one doctor to the next, hoping to find some physical cause for his perpetual weariness. But guilt, or the suppression of it, does not show up in the test tube or on the X-ray film.

It is not just the work of suppressing guilt that may leave us tired but the act of carrying guilt adds to feelings of exhaustion. Guilt is a burden that weighs heavily upon the inner person. Just as the burden of worry about the outcome of surgery faced by a loved member of the family may leave one tired, so too may the burden of guilt.

But guilt does not have to be consciously remembered to weigh heavily on us. Though lost from the conscious ability to recall at will, it may continue to be the source of inner stress, draining the body of its energies. Of course, that experience of actually forgetting is another device commonly used to hush the guilty conscience.

REPRESSION

By repression one actually forgets, banishing events beyond the ability to recall. That which is repressed cannot be brought to conscious thought by a simple act of the will. That memory which is too painful to be faced is repressed; hidden beyond normal reach in the internal memory bank of the mind. The recollection would be too much of a threat to the sense of well-being.

It is as though one faction of the fragmented self takes over a secret mission to keep from the mind certain painful memories that are damaging to one's self-concept. The specific painful memory may be compared to decaying material at the bottom of a pool. It gives off enough pollution to let a self-aware person know that something down there is quite unhealthy. But something within a fragmented self keeps moving it out of reach. Only within the most secure setting might it be permitted to rise to the surface to conscience awareness.

"Repression is an undesirable mechanism of adjustment because it is tension-producing rather than tension-reducing." The true adjustment is not really made. It is so thoroughly removed from the mind that one does not see the need to make any actual adjustment. The tension remains, doing its damage at the level of unawareness. "Direct repression is the most harmful of the mechanisms of adjustment."[1]

Though repression becomes a common but unconscious practice among adults, children can do so by conscious intent as an act of the will. In her late forties, a counselee, plagued by the feeling that she was always cold, remembered for the first time a former decision to forget. "I was about six years old. It was just a few minutes after Daddy had raped me. I was crying as he laid me down in the creek and washed the blood and mess off with the icy water. I remember thinking, 'I've got to forget this. I won't ever remember it again.' "[2] The whole experience was repressed (forgotten). But experiences, buried by repression, have a way of decaying slowly, polluting the whole pool of life's experience. Only her feelings of the icy coldness remained as the silent signal from out of the depths, keeping her aware that some old experience with anger and guilt was rotting away far below the surface, still taking a toll on her life. Unfortunately, and not surprisingly, her coldness was only one of the prices she paid for the privilege of repression. Peace bought with the price of repression is always a poor bargain.

KNOWLEDGE

Knowledge that we are not really different often serves as a relief of the sense of guilt. It is here that much of the benefit is gained in group therapy interaction and in other psychotherapeutic modes of treatment. Here also is the value in many of the popular "self-help" paperback books that line the shelves of thousands of bookstores across the land. While secret thoughts, fantasies, or desires that seem peculiar and prohibitive have a way of inducing tremendous loads of guilt, much of the terrible nature of many thoughts comes from the feeling that the thought or inclination is peculiar. Being different or unusual may sometimes be perceived as a virtue, but when the trait is unintentional, it is often perceived as a vice.

Some counselors, who have repeatedly encountered those who feel guilty for thoughts or feelings that are quite common, have considered the need for a book entitled, *And You Thought You Were Different: There Are Millions Like You.* Or it might be entitled, *The (Secret) Facts of Life.* In spite of all the college courses in psychology, and the thousands of magazine articles that have been published, every counselor still sees the amazement and disbelief on a client's face upon hearing that virtually every male has had some fleeting incestuous thoughts in relation to his mother—or daughter. We might only wonder if even God has bothered to tabulate how many people have felt guilt for the secret impulse to defecate upon the grave of a loved one. Or we could go into lengthy discussion about those millions who feel frightened and guilty for feeling they possess superhuman powers rivaling any god conceived by man.

The sense of guilt seems to dissipate when we become aware that we are not terribly different from others and we see ourselves as normal. But what one does with knowledge is of far more importance than the mere attaining of knowledge. When one is truly guilty, having truly harmed himself or others, knowledge by itself may lead to despair. Some in the helping professions have in error propagated the idea that knowledge is the only key to the resolution of all emotional conflict—including guilt. But knowledge that does not lead to constructive change often leaves a person bewildered and discouraged. Karen Horney reminds us that "an endless search for knowledge [is] valuable in itself but [is] nevertheless doomed to futility as long as the patient insists that the rays of knowledge should dispel every cloud in his life without his doing the actual changing."[3]

I have sometimes had to remind patients that they might conceivably remain in therapy for ten years and understand themselves in the most minute detail. But until they took responsible steps to change their behavior, no amount of knowledge would magically change their lives or their world.

DISTRACTIONS

Distraction is one of the most conscious devices used by men to aid in the process of escape by suppression. The blaring of the radio or concentration on television can be used to keep oneself from hearing his own accusing voice of conscience. He despises the silence for then he hears the haunting voice of failure to be or to do as he feels he ought. He strives to avoid the conflict.

Sleep is a common requirement for the mind and the body, but when it is used excessively, we have to suspect some additional motivation. Sleep rarely is suspected as a means of fleeing guilt, since guilt is so commonly recognized as a robber of sleep. It does, indeed, keep many from a night of quiet rest, but for each one it keeps awake another uses sleep as an escape from the inner accusing voice. While one person eases into the quiet, restful sleep of the innocent, another flees to the troubled, unrelaxed sleep of the guilty—a sleep not far removed from a faint.

When one complains (or others complain about him), "I don't know why, but I (or he) just can't seem to get enough sleep," a medical check-up should be required. An underactive thyroid gland or some other physical complication may be the problem. But if no physical deficiency is uncovered, a diseased conscience must be considered as a highly probable source of the problem.

Sexual intercourse or masturbation may serve effectively to divert the mind from the attack by guilt feelings. The excitement, the memories of previous sexual experiences, or the anticipation of sexual experience, can all serve much the same purpose.

When people are failing in the maintaining of interpersonal relationships, it is not uncommon for the parties to feel a deep sense of guilt. The thrill of sexual arousal momentarily blocks out the feelings of guilt associated with awareness that the relationship is not as it ought to be.

The word thrill seems to be the key to understanding this mechanism. The overall sexual experience serves as the evasive action from guilt's pursuit, but as Miller and Swanson have stated, it is within the brief moments of orgasm that the person most totally sets aside his guilt feelings and can simply enjoy the most intense pleasure that humans can experience.[4] For at least a few moments, the thrill is stronger than the sense of guilt. But when the thrill is gone, the guilt returns and if the sexual experience was a violation of the inner code of standards, the load of guilt is now larger and heavier and more stressful than before.

Crime is often a temporary thrill mechanism. Of course, like many other methods of evading the feelings of guilt, when the deed is completed, the guilt may be even stronger than before. But the thrill of plotting the crime, the enactment of the crime, and the memory of it all serve as temporary deadeners of the feelings of guilt. And they typically leave the criminal with an economic bonus for his misdeed. His ego is temporarily strengthened by having fooled the authorities. He is boosted by telling himself how smart, how cunning, how tough he is. His satisfaction tends to nullify any sense of guilt.

Intellectual pursuits serve as both escape and evasive tactics to avoid conscious awareness of guilt's torture. One can virtually drown the mind in mental activity. Concentrating on an idea or theory of one's own or of another can go to such depths that one is not at all aware of the accusing conscience. We may indeed lose ourselves in thought, wandering in a maze of either worthwhile or worthless reasonings.[5] The avid reader, the prolific writer, or the dedicated researcher, commonly seen as an intellectual, may be simply one who has learned an effective method of running from his inner accuser.

Forced mental activity such as the memorization of baseball batting averages and other relatively useless trivia are quite common escapism devices. The memorized data may be used later in an effort to gain an elevated sense of worth or status as the user impresses his peers. In addition, since an interest in athletics is commonly seen as a masculine trait in our culture, one may pump up his own sagging image of his manhood. Bear in mind that the failure to be a man is the source of some of the worst guilt feeling among men. Such mental activity then may serve at least three values: distraction from the accusing voice of conscience, inflation of the image in the eyes of others, and reassurance that one is the man he ought to be. All three may relate directly to an underlying strata of guilt.

Work in excessive amounts may be used quite effectively for the purpose of distraction. Evidence is seen repeatedly in the counselor's office pointing to distraction as a significant motive for "workaholism."[6] Busy hands and a busy mind do not have time to think about personal failings.[7]

Play is commonly used in a similar fashion and is more acceptable for those having an aversion to work. It seems more than obvious that neither work nor play are bad or destructive in themselves. It is the misuse that becomes harmful and which concerns us here. We have heard it often said of someone, "He seems to work at playing." When play is used for escape from the turmoil of guilt rather than for refreshment and revitalization, it does tend to become a toil. Thus used, one may easily overextend himself, thus defeating the re-creative benefits of recreation. Almost any form of entertainment or leisure activity is subject to this kind of abuse.

ISOLATION

Isolation, sometimes called detachment, may be considered as a form of suppression and related to repression, but is different enough to be treated separately. While isolation is the technical word used by some professionals, some feel that emotional detachment might be a better term. By cutting oneself off from the experience, he responds as if he were a nonparticipant in that which would otherwise induce pain. Isolation is used by the self to separate, by emotional barrier, an idea or an event from its affective charge of guilt.

It is a method of coping with an experience that is expected to be unbearable. Freud saw it as a rational process drawn into protective service of the ego. When isolation is used as the defense from guilt " . . . what remains in consciousness is nothing but an ideation content which is perfectly colorless and is judged to be unimportant."[8] The event is then without affect. A prostitute has written of her experiences: "The act of sex I could go through because I hardly seemed to be taking part in it. It was merely something happening to me, while my mind drifted inconsequentially away. Indeed, it was scarcely happening to me; it was happening to something lying on a bed that had a vague connection with me, while I was calculating whether I could afford a new coat or impatiently counting sheep jumping over a gate."[9]

It now seems more obvious why some much prefer the term emotional detachment to describe this method of self-defense. Such emotional withdrawal seems rather common as a flight from what would be otherwise unbearable guilt. By use of such a denying, isolating, withdrawal, the person is refusing to evaluate his own behavior. By isolation, one is repressing not the event or the source of guilt, but the value-judgment that would otherwise result in the stress-producing feelings of guilt.

MASKING

By masking, one may hide from his humiliating self-knowledge by putting on what Caryll Houselander refers to as "psychological fancy dress."

Psychological fancy dress . . . must not only give the wearer confidence and hide what shames him from others; he must hide it from himself. It must not only justify his conduct, he must glorify it. Guilty man is not content merely to excuse himself; he needs to boast; he craves the support and reassurance of his fellow men; he wants their flattery and applause, and he wants it exactly in proportion to his misgiving about himself. . . . the immoral woman will often see herself, not as degraded, but as uniquely pure and innocent, an emancipated human being, free of all the dirty little restrictions and inhibitions which contaminate the mind of the prude. . . .

She is likely to think of herself as an "enchantress" identifying herself with "one of the famous adulteresses or courtesans . . . whose sins are glorified by the vulgarity of their many envious admirers."[10]

The term, fancy dress, used by Houselander, brings to mind the fancy dress of fig leaves worn by Adam and Eve and the inadequacy of their attire that made them want to run and hide themselves from Jehovah.[11] Their need for fig leaves denoted self-awareness, and self-awareness often gives one the feeling of being seen just as one really is. "I am revealed" can give the feeling of nudity.

Nakedness is more than physical. A person confessing often gets the feeling that he is taking his clothes off in the presence of the confessor. Therapists aware of nonverbal communication will take note of a client who keeps on a coat in a warm office. The client is almost always acting out his feeling: "I have no intention of letting you see the real me today." When that client later takes off his coat, he begins to open up, more totally unveiling himself to the therapist.

Some experimental therapists have tried to capitalize on this phenomenon of common human experience and have tried nude therapy in which the patient and therapist take off all clothing at the beginning of every therapy session. In theory, if a person is undressed physically, he will find it easier to "undress" emotionally, thus more quickly revealing his inner secret conflicts. Of course, the temptation for exploitation of the patient by the therapist is more than obvious. In addition to this objection, is the fact that one physically disrobed may compensate for his physical nudity by more deeply concealing his thoughts and feelings, thus defeating the purpose, if not forcing the patient to more deeply bury his troublesome conflict.

While still on the subject of hiding, and while having been reminded of the efforts of Adam and Eve to hide themselves, we must remember that hiding is a way of trying to get out of the presence of someone. In other biblical literature, when the Apostle Peter recognized the insight of Jesus of Nazareth, he cried out to Jesus, "Depart from me, for I am a sinful man, O Lord!"[12]

The guilty person wishes to stay out of the presence of the incisive and those he sees as righteous. "The incisive might see me, and the religious further reminds me of my own failure to be as I ought." Seeing the other's righteousness often widens more fully the gap between them. The greater the gap, the greater the tendency to feel oneself as the worst of sinners, thus becoming even further alienated from others. If I am the chief of sinners, all others are cleaner or better than I. All remind me of my failures, if all are by comparison cleaner than I.

This hiding, from others or from the self in inner deception, has carried historically the title of "hypocrisy." Its roots lead one back into the ideas of covering, hiding, or stage-playacting. It is a deception of being outwardly good, but inwardly insincere. Older roots of the word suggest the wearing of a mask. Of course, like most other methods of dealing with one's destructive behavior and attitudes, it is a method that prevents a solution.[13]

FANTASY

By fantasy, possibly better known to many as day-dreaming, one may direct his mind to real or fancied events that prevent his thoughts from hearing the attack of his accuser. One's dream world seems more acceptable than the world of reality. The world of reality may be harsh, cruel, and condemning. As one person said, "Because of what I keep hearing inside me, I'd like to be able to run to a world a million miles away." Then after but a momentary pause she continued, "But even there I'd still have to be with me." When the reality of the present world hurts, it should not seem peculiar that one would prefer to flee mentally to another time and another place and state of mind.

But many feel it wrong to indulge in fantasy. Their trip then leaves them feeling even more guilty upon return to the world of the real.[14]

OPIATES

Opiates are for the numbing of feelings. Therefore, when we consider that opium is among the world's most powerful drugs for deadening pain, it seems only natural that opiates rank high on any list of escapist devices for attempting to deaden the pain of guilt. But since drugs often reduce the inner controlling ability, a person may perform acts while under the opiate influence that will leave him with added guilt.

Any reduction of distress is at least momentarily pleasurable, and drugs may induce their own kind of pleasurable experience. If that occurs, the person gets a psychological reinforcement to try the experience again. As pleasurable drug experiences are repeated, he becomes physiologically dependent upon them. It is easier to progress from there to other drugs for more satisfying reactions. Some drugs after repeated administration lead to the development of a tolerance, thus requiring a larger dose to get the same effect. The user may eventually need more than one hundred times the original amount to get the original type reaction. As the doses increase in size and number, the system may develop a physiological dependency. The body requires the drug for its normal functioning. While one has become numb to the feelings of guilt, he has become even more guilty of damaging himself.

Alcoholic beverage, also an addicting drug, has become far more socially acceptable as an opiate escape. Possibly more subtle in its addictive powers, and more socially acceptable, it is by far the most common opiate in current use in the United States. Under the guise of having fun, one can dull the painful feelings of having failed in some area of life, or even those feelings of having failed in all of life.

One may try to drown the feelings of guilt, but when sober again, the last drinking episode may be only more fuel to the fire of guilt. The desire to escape may be even stronger, thus adding compulsion to return to drink.[15] Whatever else may be involved in the alcoholic's plight, the struggle with guilt is virtually always a part of motivation.

INSANITY

Insanity is usually among the last resorts to which one may turn to escape the haunting conscience. Though normally an unconscious choice, the desperate may remark, "I feel that I have only two choices left. I can either go crazy or I can kill myself."

At this point, the concern is not with the level of consciousness or unconsciousness that the choice is made. The simple fact stands that insanity, a psychotic break with reality, is often an adjusting mechanism used to escape the pain of guilt.[16] One expression of insanity, the flight to grandeur, may not be so much a delusion of greatness as it is a delusion of goodness.[17] I remember a patient who proclaimed himself to be the "Father of God Almighty." Few saw the significance of his passing statement, "I am the good one." Most wished to evaluate his need for power. In one's reaction against seeing himself so terribly bad, he may see himself as Jesus Christ or God, or the Father of God —not "all great" but "all good."

But insanity itself may be another source of guilt. Regaining contact with reality, he may have enough recollection of his former behavior to feel ashamed and guilty. "I ought to have behaved differently." Any peculiar behavior of the seriously mentally ill may have this effect. "I ought to have been able to make a more healthy adjustment."[18]

No matter what the degree of success one has in escaping the pursuing accuser, he follows close behind with implements of torture in hand.

EVASION OF GUILT FEELINGS

Nobody envies a man on the run. Instead, we are likely to pity him and identify with him. In our minds we see him watching over his shoulder, or cowering in a dark corner. His sleep is listless. He is wide-eyed at the slightest noise. If he finds a haven, his stomach knots at every knock on the door, his palms are sweaty, and his hands tremble.

Or we picture a lone airman shot down behind enemy lines, grubbing for roots and snails. He hears the bark of a family pet in the distance, and suspects a bloodhound has picked up his trail. He quickens his pace and wonders if he would even hear the crack of the rifle if a bullet found its mark. He hears a series of thundering booms and stops short in his tracks. It is the pounding of his heart drumming in his ears. He hides under a thick bush until darkness when he can move on. He's confused. Which way does he go? He's hungry. Is he about to run straight back into the hands of the enemy? Would he have the ability to withstand torturous interrogation? Should he let himself be taken alive? Should he kill himself and get it over with?

The ordinary man who works five days a week, struggles to meet the mortgage payments, and frets over the crab grass in the front lawn, may be as much a man on the run as the man we have just described. But this man is trying to elude the pursuing sense of guilt. His course is somewhat open. He can choose from a number of routes in his evasive efforts.

SUBLIMATION

Sublimation is an alternate gratification, and one of the few positive forms of evading guilt. In order to understand the practice of sublimation, we must first understand that one may feel just as guilty for his impulses as he feels for things he actually does. Sublimation is as true an evasive practice as one would see. In sublimation one modifies the fulfillment of a forbidden urge in such a way as to make it acceptable. He discharges the urge by substitute activity. For instance, the man who is inclined to build a clandestine relationship with a woman of his acquaintance, instead, goes home and works to build a better relationship with his wife.

Some would suggest that sublimation ought not be included as a defense mechanism since it is a way of avoiding a guilt-producing activity. It reminds us that one can know fully before the fact that he will feel guilty if he participates in a forbidden act. Sublimation, therefore, anticipates the fact and provides gratification in an acceptable behavior. It moves us to more constructive action. It is not surprising, therefore, that sublimation is recognized as the defense mechanism in which there is no damage to the personality. It is one of the most constructive, complete, and successful of the defense mechanisms for dealing with guilt.[1]

OVERREACTION

Overreaction goes by the technical name of "reaction formation." It is an additional means of evading guilt in anticipation of an act. It is a response to a forbidden impulse. It is the countering of the impulse with the opposite; a means of keeping oneself from putting his own unconscious desires into action.

A child asked why a certain man had given his entire life in a personal crusade against the consumption of alcoholic beverage. Some responded that it was quite possible that the crusader had a strong impulse to abuse the use of alcoholic beverage and this was his way of defending himself against it. Right or wrong about that particular person, it does show a common awareness to the use of this form of defense. "He who doth protest too strongly" is often suspect of using this defense, whether against the use of alcoholic beverage, against homosexuality, obscene literature or some other impulse that would produce intense guilt *if even the desire were admitted* to the self.

Unfortunately, one engaging in a reaction formation often assumes a repulsive, self-righteous stance. His pharisaism is often thinly veiled and recognized by the observer. The constant preoccupation with the moralism reveals the unconscious eagerness.

For this reason the social do-gooder is often resented. He is suspected of being, not so genuinely concerned with the welfare of others as he is with his own welfare and his own defenses against hidden, forbidden impulses. If the layman's observation concerning the antialcoholic beverage crusader mentioned above was correct, his crusade would not have been genuinely for the best interests of the public but for preservation of his own self-image.

Lest one get the idea that only the public crusader for

morality may use this form of defense, remember that many use the mechanism self-destructively. For instance, the Don Juanian type behavior may be used by one fleeing his highly guilt-producing homosexual impulses.

DENIAL OF STANDARDS

Denial of the existence of true standards is highly popular among the more educationally sophisticated as a method of guilt reduction. Coleman[2] and Horney[3] both write of the practice. A common argument says, "All right and wrong is purely dependent upon the particular culture in question. Rules for conduct are totally relative." It is easy then to compare some petty teachings of one culture over against those of another. The speaker may then add that none should ever feel guilty, since all standards are relative. And he then may ask why anyone would live up to a standard just for the sake of the standard. On the surface, the position sounds quite reasonable.

But more than the wording of a standard is at stake! People are being truly harmed! Are we to believe that it is a cultural influence that says that a nine-year-old girl should not be raped? Is it a regional culture taboo that forces us to cry out in rage when a five-year-old boy is tied to a tree, burned repeatedly with cigarettes, and then strangled?

WILLY LOMANISM

Refusal to form a code, sometimes called "Willy Lomanism"[4] or "fixation," is a way of remaining a perpetual child. In childhood, expectations come from others: parents, siblings, friends, and the general culture in which the person is developing. The only person who might possibly exist without standards would be that humanoid creature, the feral child, reared in the wilds by animals. Some would assume that such a "person" would have had no expectations placed on him by others. He would therefore feel no sense of guilt. If we think about it, we cannot help but raise at least two questions. First, is it not possible that the animals themselves might communicate to the growing child *their* expectations of him? It seems somewhat doubtful that he would be able to live up to them entirely. But is it not possible, or is it not even probable, that he would expect to be able to run as fast, climb as swiftly, or burrow as deeply as his companions? If he expected himself to do so, but were not able, he would be failing in his own expectations, and we know that a sense of failure equals the sense of guilt.

Study of written material on the subject clearly shows that most students of human behavior insist that the normal process of becoming more human requires the building of one's own inner code of expectation. This is part of the process of becoming a person. Without such an internalized code, one is something less than a complete personality. The mature personality says, in essence, "Regardless of what others say or think, here I stand; this is what I expect of me." But some refuse this significant step. Dennis Geaney writes:

There are some people who never go through their adolescence and who spend their lives conforming to the wishes of others. Willy Loman, who lived his life to please others was morally a child. He never operated from a core or center of gravity within himself. He was pathetic because he did not assume responsibility for life. What others thought and expected of him became his golden rule.[5]

By fixating, one seems to reason, "If I don't form rules to live by, I don't violate them. Therefore, I won't feel guilty." But shuffling through life in his codeless immaturity, he will invariably injure himself and others around him again and again and again.

REGRESSION

Regression is most simply defined as growth in reverse. In the face of excessive guilt, a person may quickly grow backward to a period of less conflict with inner expectations. His feelings of inadequacy and helplessness, in the face of his guilt-producing failures, urge him back to a period when he had fewer expectations of himself. If he is less mature, neither he nor those around him expect as much of him.

The major difference between regression and fixation mentioned earlier, is that in fixation one ceases to mature at a period of development. In regression one has gone on toward more mature development but returns at a later time to an earlier level of immaturity.

Dr. George Kisker points to the use of regression as a method of reducing guilt feelings amid the problem of homosexuality. He reminds us that any overt heterosexual relationship, in some persons, is highly guilt-producing. The person of the opposite sex is too holy or too pure to be tainted by the sexual relationship. When the heterosexual relationship is too guilt provoking, one regresses. "Since strong attachments to members of the same sex is characteristic of the early phase of adolescence, an individual may find later in life that it is easier to adjust emotionally to this earlier level than to the level of mature sexuality where heterosexual relations are expected."[6]

But since homosexuality is commonly a source of guilt also, it seems more evident that many mechanisms of adjustment to guilt are choices that involve what seems to the person to be the lesser of two evils. The mechanisms often do not eliminate the sense of guilt, but the mechanism is used at least to reduce the sense of guilt. The attitude seems to be, "less is better than a lot." The major problem with this attitude, however, is that the guilt is simply spread out into several sources instead of centered on one source. Though more evenly distributed it is still there and the mechanism chosen may eventually compound the original sense of guilt!

DENIAL

Denial, in some form, is probably one of the most common means of evading the feelings of guilt. Virtually all of this chapter and much of the entire book could be legitimately classified as some form of denial. One may gossip, lie, cheat, or treat his fellow man in any number of harmful ways, but he sees himself as nice in comparison to others around him who are more terrible. Some people will not admit the existence of evil in themselves; they will not, and perhaps ultimately cannot allow the dark of their nature to invade their consciousness. They refuse to know it. They have formed a superhuman ideal of themselves and will not countenance the possibility of frailty and sensuality within them even as a potentiality.[7] Denying any wrongdoing, there is nothing to change nor any reason for change. There is no reason to improve. Speaking from a religious perspective, Bishop Fulton Sheen has said:

There has been no single influence which has done more to prevent man from finding God and rebuilding his character, has done more to lower the moral tone of society than the denial of personal guilt.[8]

The practice of denial can be carried to almost any degree of human struggle. Carol Murphy has written of an extreme case incorporating repression into denial:

A woman, committed to a mental hospital, tried to kill herself and her children. Her children died, but she survived, with total amnesia for the tragedy. She had rejected the fact of what she had done, and had, therefore, rejected the sense of guilt. But it was her guilt that made the memory of her deed unbearable.[9]

Police are well experienced with those who try to use denial to evade any sense of guilt for their behavior. A man may plant a bomb in a public building where scores of lives may be endangered. Before the bomb is timed to explode, he may try to relieve his sense of guilt by calling in a warning. His reasoning seems to follow the course: "They know of the danger. They should get out of the building. If people are harmed, it is really their fault." He, therefore, denies accepting any sense of moral responsibility for those injured.

Even if we are not denying reality, others are ready to assist us in doing so. In February 1978 civic leaders in Akron, Ohio, considered an ordinance that would require abortion clinics to show photographs of a fetus at approximately the age of the one about to be aborted. Some reports alleged that people objecting to the ordinance were against the use of the words "unborn child" and objected to the viewing of the photographs because they would stir guilt in the woman if she proceeded with the abortion.

Many of those advocating more liberal use of abortion have insisted that women usually come through the experience guilt free. They show personality surveys to prove their point, which should not surprise anyone. The woman is likely to have gathered virtually every defense mechanism at her disposal to protect herself against feeling guilty. As long as the refortified defenses stand, she will not feel the sense of guilt. But since defenses do often crumble, sometimes fifteen to twenty-five years after an experience of this magnitude, some therapists are uneasy in anticipation of an avalanche of guilt-ridden clients in the years ahead. Denial or any other defense will not necessarily go on forever.

IGNORANCE

Ignorance serves as a haven amid a storm. "I didn't know the gun was loaded," ran the lines of a song of the 1940s. But a friend lay injured. The logic goes, "Since I did not know, I am not responsible." Lack of awareness that a behavior would bring harm to another tends to relieve guilt, since intent was lacking. "I thought you had walked away," a parent may tell his child after having slammed a door on the child's finger. "I didn't do it on purpose." When no design to harm exists, one may feel relieved, unless he asks himself, "But were you not responsible to learn if the gun were loaded before you pulled the trigger," or "Ought you not to have kept an eye on your child?" The feeling of failure to have acted more responsibly thus compounds the sense of guilt.

PERFECTIONISM

Perfectionism has been called the vain search for glory. It says, "Forget about the disgraceful creature you really *are*; this is how you should be; and to be this idealized self is all that matters."[10] Oddly enough, the person using this tactic does not aim at real change in his behavior. Since the judgment of others is a major source of what we usually call guilt feelings, his aim is to give the appearance of absolute perfection. But one quickly believes his own act. Such an individual's perfection for honesty, or fairness, or compassion, does not produce a true striving for honesty, or fairness, or compassion, but produces only a drive to attain absoluteness in these qualities, which is, of course, always just around the corner or is attained in the imagination.[11] They are not true moral standards to be achieved. They are only empty ideals.

RIGID RIGHTNESS

"I'm always right" covers the danger of feeling altogether wrong. It is an impenetrable defense. It protects from criticism from within as well as from without. The man who is always right or perfect leaves no possible hole for criticism to find penetration. No reason, nor logic will get through. The most glaring wrong will be neither seen nor heard. The most irrational logic will be used to justify and defend the most blatant injustice. "The attitude may go so far as to make it necessary to be right in the most insignificant and trifling details—to be always right about the weather,"[12] or the outcome of last week's football game, for example.

DEFENSIVE AGGRESSION

Defensive aggression is precisely that suggested by the name; a label used to describe the behavior of one aggressively defending himself. When he is reminded of his guilt, he turns in anger to attack the person who reminds him of his failure. The anger felt for himself he directs toward another. He can accept anger more easily than he can accept the pain of guilt. The anger hides the feelings of guilt, not only covering as a smoke screen, but momentarily nullifying them.

This kind of reaction to guilt may be seen in the day-to-day interchanges within a family. The husband who feels aggressive toward his wife, annoyed and provoked by trivialities, could appropriately ask himself, "What have I done wrong toward her?"[13] Honesty with himself will usually provide an answer. A concerned parent may sit down with his child to discuss an act of misbehavior only to be countered by the child's agressive outburst.[14] He is not only defending himself against the parent. He is defending himself against himself. Reminded of his guilt, he has become defensively aggressive against the assault upon his self-esteem.

HATE THE HARMED

To hate the harmed may seem at first to be a reversal of words. Few would question the fact that we have a tendency to harm those we hate, but it is not so generally recognized that we may just as likely hate those we have harmed. George Clark, editor of *Church Administration Magazine*, was the first to call this to my attention, but it was Abraham Ross of the University of Minnesota who keenly observed this phenomenon of human behavior in clinically controlled settings. His studies conclude that with "no means of restitution available to a person, he will derogate the harmed person as a means of reducing his (sense of) guilt."[15] He must find fault in the person he has harmed or he must create fault (in his own mind) to make the harmed person into such a terrible creature that he truly deserves to be harmed. Anyone would be justified in harming such a despicable person.

The marriage counselor does not have far to look to

see this dynamic in action in those who seek his services. A husband who has deeply wounded his wife may immediately begin to find fault, or create fault in his own mind, concluding that his wife is truly worthy of contempt and the injury she has suffered. He feels justified in having inflicted it upon her.

SCAPEGOATING

Scapegoating, often called projection, is used when someone assigns his own guilt to another. The person sees guilt in himself and projects it onto some other person. "See the look in his eye. Look at his face. Obviously, he's evil." Using projection as a system of defense makes it easy for someone to hate another person without even knowing him. Using scapegoating, one can reject or even harm another person he projects as "deserving it" and come away feeling pure. Houselander has said:

"There is hardly an evil force more terrible than projected self-hatred. It is not for nothing we are told to love *our neighbors* as ourself, *we must tremble lest refusing to come to terms with* all *that is self, we hate our neighbor as ourself. . . . A classic story is told of Hitler who, when visiting a village where one of the cruelest purges had been carried out, wept bitterly, saying, 'How wicked these people must be, to have made me do this!'* "[16]

When one assigns his guilt to another, there is no end to the cruelty he may inflict that would otherwise be directed toward the self.

Blame the Mirror is possibly the truest form of projection. The form of behavior is comparable to a man attacking a mirror, but in this case the mirror is another person. One sees reflected in the other the faults he cannot bear to admit seeing in himself. He attacks the other person who has his own, or similar faults.[17] Jesus of Nazareth spoke clearly to the practice:

And why do you look at the speck in your brother's eye, but do not notice the log that is in your own eye? Or how can you say to your brother, "Let me take the speck out of your eye," and behold, the log is in your own eye?
You hypocrite, first take the log out of your own eye; and then you will see clearly enough to take the speck out of your brother's eye.[18]

The anger a man feels for himself, he commonly directs toward another. He again becomes aggressive in his defense of himself. The attacker's blindness to his own faults make him quite "pharisaical" or self-righteous. If the one reproached sees the irony he might respond, "You are like the pot calling the kettle black."

There is some unhealthy comfort in seeing another as lower than oneself. "I am cleaner or better than that person." "Cleaner" is momentarily experienced as "clean." "Better" is momentarily experienced as "good." Thus, the embezzler looks down on the confidence man who looks down on the burglar who looks down on the call girl who looks down on the streetwalker who looks down on the pimp who looks down on the child molester, etc., etc. Each momentarily experiences the feeling of being "clean" and "good." Each one "below" helps the one "above" by giving the one above the feeling that the one below is a little more degraded than he.[19]

Pass the buck, another form of scapegoating says, "Don't blame me. Somebody else made me do it." I'm a victim. Here one tries to deny responsibility for his own actions by placing the responsibility on someone else. In the more conscious form of scapegoating one admits the behavior, but contends he was forced by circumstances or by someone else. After having harmed someone he may, with the speed of lightning, switch to feeling abused.

His terror of wrongdoing simply compels him to feel himself the victim, even when in actual fact he has been the one who failed others or who, through his implicit demands, has imposed on them. Because feeling victimized thus becomes a protection against his self-hate, it is a strategical position, to be defended vigorously.[20]

Karen Horney was convinced that this is the single "most effective" defense against self-recrimination.[21] It "makes him inaccessible to help for the time being. For to accept help . . . would cause the defensive position of his being altogether the victim to collapse."[22]

During the early part of the 1970s the comedian, Flip Wilson, repeatedly brought laughter to millions with his properly-timed line, "The Devil made me do it!" The humor seems to have come from the commonly recognized absurdity revealed in the remark so often used among Americans. It seems to touch the nonsensical denial of reality common to many of us.

Men want to blame everyone but themselves for their faults. A young woman, struggling with her guilty conscience for a sexual indiscretion commented, "He led me on. And he said that I could prove my love for him only by letting him do it. It wasn't really my fault." A boy in trouble with the police responded, "The fellows really made me do it. They said that I was 'chicken' if I didn't steal the hubcaps off that car."

Some schools of deterministic psychology have added to the problem. They have thoroughly removed blame from the person who actually performed a misdeed and laid it upon parents, grandparents, neighbors, and communities. The whole society was blamed when a 180-pound boy beat and robbed a ninety-pound, eighty-five-year-old widow in a parking lot. When a young thug raped a sixteen-year-old girl the judge blamed the permissive society and released the rapist. Reason and common sense seem to have gone out the window when such culprits are said to be only the product of the society and that it is the society that needs changing and not the person who performed the attack. Such illogic pandered by the renowned pseudo-intellectuals temporarily salves the consciences of the truly guilty and makes it easier for them to return to their loathsome deeds. "Even the people who are supposed to know say it's the society that makes me do these things."

Since Freud we have assumed that "insight" into the forces that have molded our personalities is a good and health-producing experience. The goal has been the age old proverb: "Know thyself." However, the irony of it has been that many times this has led to the "insight" that it is someone's fault that we have turned out as we have and that we act or feel as bad as we do. The longer we have talked in therapy, the longer has grown the list of those culprits who are responsible *for our own disordered lives.*[23]

A historic example of this "I'm not to blame" pattern of thinking occurred when Adolf Hitler blamed the Jews for forcing World War II upon the Germans. In a letter he wrote just before he died, he stated:

It is true that neither I, nor anybody else in Germany, wanted war in 1939. It was wanted and provoked exclusively by those international politicians who either came of Jewish stock or worked for Jewish interests. After all my efforts of disarmament posterity cannot place the responsibility for this war on me.[24]

His followers seem to have generally adopted the same line of thought. Having herded millions of Jews into the gas chambers, during the War Crimes Trials, they almost invariably blamed the higher-ups whom they had obeyed without question.

When the Devil or society or superiors or peers have not been blamed in efforts to displace responsibility, God has been blamed. A man downed a fifth of whiskey, raced his car down the street onto the sidewalk, and killed two kindergarten children. Even the people of the local churches tried to lift the responsibility from the irresponsible driver. "I don't understand it but the Lord doesn't make mistakes." Somebody else responded, "I don't understand it either. The Lord must have been trying to teach their parents something." *Almost no one spoke of the responsibility of the drunken driver!*

A man watches the tires wear slick on his car. When one blows out, causing an accident that kills a member of his family, he calls it "an act of God," or he shifts responsibility to God saying that his loved one's "days were numbered." For those things for which men want to displace responsibility, they freely blame God or the forces of the devil to help escape the pangs of guilt. A student brought in the following lines attributed to Anna Russell:

At three, I had the feeling of ambivalence toward my brothers,
And so it follows naturally I poison all my lovers.

But I am happy; how I've learned the lesson this has taught;
That everything I do that's wrong is someone else's fault.[25]

The concept of scapegoating has almost totally reversed in its meaning since its origin in ancient Hebrew religion. The guilty Jewish nation was admitting (confessing) their own moral failure in the ceremony—not blaming the goat. They looked to the goat to symbolize the carrying away of their sin. It was symbolically laid upon the goat which was left to wander into the open wilderness. Modern men often skip the confession and move directly to laying the blame on anything or anyone within reach. No person or group has a corner on the practice. While the acknowledged thief lays the blame for his theft on the social conditions, people of the church may lay the moral blame upon the pastor for the church's failure to reach its budget.

SUBSTITUTION

People often substitute things for relationships in making adjustment to guilt. A woman, lamenting the relationship with her husband wept, "I have a safety deposit box full of diamonds, a Mercedes and a Cadillac in the garage, and more furs and dresses than I can ever wear. My husband has never been able to understand that instead of all those *things,* I just want him." While he may be making an atoning payment for his guilt in this relationship, it seems that he is using things in substitution for affection and time. He does not give them instead of his love, but as his only expression of love. But she is receiving the substitute he offers so he won't feel guilty.

UNDOING

Undoing sounds illogical—and it is. But we are not discussing logic. We are discussing the things people do to escape the emotional pain of guilt. It is not at all unusual for one to participate in an "undoing" effort.

Undoing has been called a "negative magic."[26] It is so named because it seems to magically abolish behavior that has been completed. The term is not at all uncommon in psychoanalytic literature and is usually associated with some form of ritual. "Rituals of sacrifice, atonement, lustrations, and baptism may be expected magically to undo the sinfully broken relationship, or (undo) the prescribed sin which has been performed."[27] One adopting the undoing mechanism of adjustment is using a thought pattern similar to my patient who said, "If I refuse to believe I have had a heart attack, I will not have had a heart attack." This was in the face of full medical evidence that the heart muscle had most certainly been damaged. It is as though one is saying at some level within himself, "If I go through a certain thought process or through a certain ritual often enough, or suffer enough, or pay enough, not only can I make it *as though* it never happened, *I can eventually erase the misdeed from history.* It will never have been."

DISPLACEMENT

Displacement is a term commonly reserved for use in discussion of aggression, but Sidney Jordan shows the use of displacement in successful reduction of guilt feelings. He points out that one may reduce the feelings of guilt for some major misdeed by displacing guilt disproportionately toward some minor omission or deed. For instance, if one has cheated for several years on his income tax, having displaced his feelings of guilt, he may feel extremely guilty for forgetting to pay the paperboy,[28] while feeling relatively innocent in relation to the tax cheat. He uses it to tone down the sense of guilt. Using displacement one says, in effect, "O.K. I'm guilty. But not for much."[29]

RATIONALIZATION

Rationalization is the intellectual mode of escape. It is the selection of an explanation which will preserve the self-esteem that would otherwise be lost by awareness of guilt. It is a form of self-deception. Hensie and Campbell have said that "a person 'covers up,' justifies, [or] rationalizes an act or an idea that is unreasonable or illogical."[30]

Redl and Wineman studied a group of delinquent and aggressive children who rationalized their actions, without guilt feelings, in the following manner:

"He did it first."

"Everybody else does such things, anyway."

"We were all in on it."

"But somebody else did that same thing to me before."

"He had it coming to him."

"I had to do it, or I would have lost face."

"I didn't use the proceeds anyway."

"But I made up with him afterwards."

"He is a no-good so-and-so himself."

"They are all against me, nobody likes me, they are always picking on me."

"I couldn't have gotten it any other way."[31]

We might further refer to rationalization as the excuses one offers to himself or to another to explain his behavior and why he really is not guilty of misconduct. It is, of course, another form of dishonesty;

another form of denial of reality. But the unconscious mind cannot accept rationalization. "We may convince ourselves at the intellectual level but not at the emotional and spiritual level. The inner self knows better!"[32] It knows the truth!

JUSTIFICATION

Justification is sometimes referred to as a form of rationalization. One rationalizes to justify himself. He is trying to stay in good standing with himself or another.[33] It has often been said that one rarely does anything he considers "wrong" until he first justifies it in his own mind—good reason rather than real reasons for what he does. A salesman who has really failed to explore a newly opened market may try to justify his sales decline by finding and magnifying a fault in his good product. A man may even kill by justifying himself, either before or after the fact. "Because of the given circumstances, I can do that which I might not otherwise do." "Of course, I killed him. He was no good."

But who can fully justify his own behavior? One's own efforts to do so are always incomplete. No one knows his own motivating inner forces well enough to fully justify himself. The person mentioned above, who had killed and offered his justification in his own behalf, was not aware that he had deeper feelings of hatred for persons in authority. A still later analysis of the killer revealed that he has a hidden homosexual drive for the man whom he killed. But he was too threatened by such feelings to face them at the time. The man he killed may indeed have been a scoundrel, but his true motivation for killing was to eliminate the source of his hidden homosexual conflict and to eliminate a figure of hated authority.

Christian theologians make frequent reference to justification. It is held that no man can fully justify himself and that if justification is to be accomplished, it will have to be done by the all-knowing, but loving God of heaven and earth. It follows then that when one rationalizes to justify himself, his rationalization is a perversion of true justification. Christian theologians see self-justification directly opposed to confession. The basic meaning of the word *confess* is "to agree with," so that when one confesses to God, he is agreeing with God; "You are correct. I have done wrong when I harmed myself or another." When confession is made as an act of faith, a condition is fulfilled in preparation for forgiveness and reconciliation. Since a man cannot know himself well enough to justify himself, Christianity encourages the man to trust God to do for him that which he cannot do for himself. Only an all-knowing and loving God can truly justify him, giving him a right standing with God and with himself.

Whether one does or does not adhere to the view of the Christian faith one must concede that it is the rare occasion in which one may fully justify his own behavior. But he tries.

IDENTIFICATION

Identification in its classic form is the incorporation and integration of the personality traits of another into the self. The process usually takes place at unconscious levels. Identification, as it relates to efforts to evade guilty responsibility, is another irrational effort to justify one's behavior and occurs nearer the conscious level. One may temporarily identify himself with a person of renown or with one whom he holds in high esteem and says, "If that behavior is all right for him, it is all right for me. If it is all right for the President or for the movie idol, there is no wrong in it for me," as if hiding under the identification of the more prominent personality.

Another form of identification is more closely related to the more classical "psychological" definitions of identification. It requires the exercise of a lot of mental and emotional gymnastics. Here, an individual incorporates within himself a mental picture of some other person. He then thinks, feels, and acts as he conceives that person to think, feel, and act. This is seen in the child who has learned immoral behavior from his parents. The child who has grown up watching his parents obtain most of his clothing by shoplifting will have a built-in defense against feeling guilty for duplicating their behavior as he too naturally steals. He may imagine himself to be not himself but his parent. He sees not himself stealing but his parent stealing. As long as he maintains that identification, he personally feels innocent.

This phenomenon is somewhat comparable to one who puts on a mask and identifies himself as being the person whose face he wears. He steals as that person. When the mask is removed, it was the other person who stole. He walks away with no sense of guilt.

CHANCE

The element of chance is probably most easily illustrated by a principle applied in an execution before a firing squad. If ten men make up the firing squad, only one will likely have a "live" bullet in the rifle. The others will have only a blank. They each choose the rifle from the rack. Each aims directly at the heart and fires. The one man kills. But all ten members to the firing squad walk away feeling relatively innocent. "The odds were ten to one. There is little likelihood that I'm the one who killed him."

DILUTION

Dilution by group participation has its similarities to the evasion of feelings of guilt by "chance." This too is a means of trying to avoid guilt in anticipation of the experience. A most obvious illustration of this type of effort to avoid guilt is seen in mob action. Murders have been committed as each member of the mob has made one stab of a knife, fired one bullet into a body, or thrown one stone. The guilt having been diluted, each member may walk away feeling, "My one little part probably wasn't enough to have killed him." Everyone comes away just a little bit guilty, but no one comes away feeling *very* guilty.

As Karl Menninger expressed it, "If a group of people can be made to share the responsibility for what would be a sin if an individual did it, the load of guilt rapidly lifts from the shoulders of all concerned. Others may accuse, but the guilt shared by the many evaporates for the individual."[34]

APPROVAL

Approval is the effort to gain acceptance of an attitude or action by someone who is seen as a keeper of the ethic; an authority on morality. Those in religious leadership roles are approached with, "It was all right that I did as I did, wasn't it?" Or, more directly, "Tell me that what I did was all right." They are really pleading, "Relieve my sense of guilt." The priest or gospel minister is seen by many as speaking directly as the voice of God, and the minister's approval is heard as equivalent to the approval of God.

Any significant authority may fill the need. Efforts to legalize abortion found much of their motivation coming out of the need for guilt reduction. "If we can get the law of the land to say that abortion is all right, there is nothing wrong in having an abortion," exemplifies the attitude that seeks to relieve the sense of guilt by approval of some authority.

CONCLUSION

Little constructive change takes place as long as we use any of the avenues of escape or evasion of the truth. When we do, we are sometimes guilty of harming persons—others or ourselves. With few exceptions, even the coping methods used to relieve guilt feelings are self-defeating. But they are all chosen as *survival techniques.* As Menninger said of men's coping devices:

Some . . . are properly classified as sins. They are aggressive, expensive, unpleasant, hurtful, even obnoxious, but they are all to some degree lifesavers for the actor! Whether sin or crime or symptom, every one of these devices represents an automatically chosen lesser evil, and an attempt to make the best bargain possible. Given the experiences of the particular individual, the set of psychological structures in his personality, the environmental situation as he perceives it, the stresses felt and the choices open to him, his strange act seemed to him "a good thing at the time"–indeed the only right thing at the time. But most of these compromises and decisions are made without much involvement of consciousness or reason. . . . Self-preservation is everybody's motive every minute, all the time, but so is a trend toward self-destruction. These two drives are in constant operation and opposition. Because of them we are constantly and continuously trying both to self-destroy and to self-preserve, to stay alive in spite of ourselves.[35]

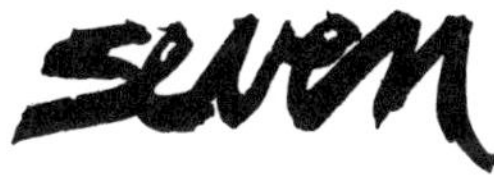

GUILT UNDER CAMOUFLAGE

Crimes against human personalities such as those mentioned in chapter 1 still go on. And when we look around us to the heartache and sorrow brought by misbehavior, it is quite evident that a lot of people are still guilty of harming one another and themselves. Now, having read through a catalogue of more than three dozen tactics commonly used to escape, evade, and defend oneself from the feelings of guilt, we can see why many feel almost no conscious sense of guilt at all. We can see more clearly also that man is truly a master of deceit—quite skilled at the art of camouflage, able to deceive even himself. But the problem is far from resolved.

Guilt can be likened to a man who goes to a masquerade ball and spends the evening repeatedly changing masks and giving clues to his identity by an elaborate game of charades. Some of the guests are puzzled throughout the evening. Some occasionally suspect his identity. And others see through his thin veil and recognize him, but continue to play his game, pretending to see nothing more than the mask he wears.

If he suspects that some recognize him, he jeers,

"Only a fool or a fanatic, or at best one lacking psychological sophistication would think I even exist." Since no one wants to be seen as a fool or a religious fanatic or one ignorant of psychological profundities, people glance uneasily at one another and agree that the word "guilt" suggests responsibility and that a man is never really responsible for his behavior since that is determined by how he was treated in childhood. Therefore, no one is ever truly guilty of anything.

And as for the feelings of guilt—those are purely anxiety reactions in the face of the loss of love. Those are just bad feelings stirred up by authority figures in their efforts to maintain control.

What, then, are those "bad feelings"? What *is* the mask of guilt? What does it look like? When it conceals itself so well, how might we, without mistake, identify it? Perhaps all the questions will not be answered to our total satisfaction, but we can find some partial answers.

Several studies, some that have resulted in a few good books, have been presented in recent years on the subject of "stress." Unfortunately, relatively little has been said about the stress produced by failing to live up to one's own adopted code of ethics. But when we examine stress carefully there is guilt, hiding among a lot of other sources of stress, hoping not to be seen. It can often do its damage without ever being noticed. Indeed, no one may ever know it is around. It is easily concealed in the source of the tension headache or heart disease. We would rather bundle it into the "tensions-of-modern-day-living" and leave it at that.

We should remember that one of the best places to hide is in a large crowd. Stress, for instance, may be the crowd with a thousand different faces. While some few people may live with only one source of stress, most of us find it coming from hundreds of different directions. And sometimes they all seem to come at once. The same thing could be said for guilt's other hiding places. Just as it would be foolish to suggest that all stress comes from guilt, it would be just as foolish to suggest that all the other hiding places conceal only guilt.

Guilt often prefers to hide under the cover of "nervousness." In many social settings, it is relatively easy to admit that one has bad nerves without ever questioning just what it is that produces such miserable feelings. In fact, it can easily be dismissed as an inherited trait. "I guess I got it from Mother." That even helps give it the sound of a communicable disease which one is totally unable to avoid. That means there is no reason to try to do anything about it.

Look into the face of depression and examine its character. No, guilt is not depression's only feature, but as often as not, guilt is there acting as a thief, taking the sparkle from the eyes, leaving a frown and the corners of the mouth turned down. Look for it also in the wards of mental hospitals.

Look behind the words that reflect low self-esteem and the sense of worthlessness. Look into the miserable feeling of anxiety that says something terrible is about to happen. Look also into 60 to 85 percent of the general hospital beds of America where psycho-physiogenic (psychosomatic, emotionally-triggered) illnesses range from peptic ulcers to cancer. While there, don't forget to look at accident-proneness.

Look into that general feeling of "not-OKness' to which Thomas Harris called the world's attention.[1] Examine the "nobody-loves-me" routine. Look into the "Doctor, I'm-as-tired-in-the-morning-when-I-wake-up-as-I-was-when-I-went-to-bed" syndrome. Look behind those feelings of irritability that the youngsters sometimes call the "grumpies."

Peek into parental overprotectiveness. Look under parental indulgences, when children are permitted to do almost anything they wish to do or are given almost anything material they ask for. Look into unresolved griefs that are still causing trouble after the passage of many years.

Look also into the life of that person who seems one day to cry for love and the next day to force rejection, who pulls you toward him with the right hand and pushes you away with the left. His "love" for you often places such a heavy demand on you that you want to run. This person operates out of guilt and tries to manipulate you with your own sensitivities to guilt.

The more we study the many hiding places and the masks of guilt, the more we realize that it can be concealed in almost any facet of life. I insist that it is among the most common, the most powerful, and the most unhealthy motivating forces of mankind. It is one of the most profound forces influencing man's feelings and one of the most compelling forces influencing his behavior toward something better, or toward something worse—even death.

GUILT REVEALED

In this book so far we have talked about the conflict going on within the self. We have dealt with expectations of the self. We first talked about harmful, pro-death behavior by the self and then about efforts at reducing the pain of guilt feelings. We have dealt with only occasional hints of judgment from outside such as a judgment coming from parents, the police, neighbors, peers, or from anyone else. The entirety of this presentation has dealt with one's tendency to judge himself and his own behavior.

All we have discussed so far has supposed the development of a behavioral code that had fed into it the *expectations* of peers, parents, other authority figures and the hundreds of other rather subtly communicated expectations or standards for behavior. Others have suggested various aspects of the code, but the behavior standard is integrated and adopted by each person individually. We have so far placed no guilt in terms of the violation of a religious expectation. Nothing has been said so far of any religious morality that would suggest expectations from a concept of a god. Nathaniel Branden insists that when a person betrays his own standards, he acquires a sense of some unknown danger, some unknown retribution, waiting for him ahead. He adds:

> *It would be a gross error to interpret this attitude as merely a consequence of the influence of religion. The issue is much wider and deeper. It arises . . . from man's* implicit *awareness that he cannot live successfully without* some *long-range principles to guide his life.* [1]

Problems arise when man violates these principles, because the violation works to bring about his destruction. Each pro-death activity makes the personality less than it was before. Anything that reduces oneself or another person makes the offender truly guilty. And that which makes one actually guilty, the New Testament commonly equates with "sin." Of course, the mention of the word "sin" immediately places the subject in a religious setting.

Many proponents of Christianity tenaciously insist that a behavior is wrong solely because Jehovah said to do or not to do a particular act, while many others would offer rather strong evidence that it may have been the other way around. When Jehovah wanted to provide a pattern of behavior that would be most constructive (pro-life) for mankind, he called attention to that pro-life behavior, and asked men to live by it. Any behavior that was pro-death was labeled "sin," "immoral," or "evil."

Men often fear the punishment of their god, when the god most to be feared is the petty *little god that men make of themselves.*[2] The definition of a *god* used here is "that to which absolute authority of supreme value is assigned." When the inner defense against guilt breaks down, the inner god demands a payment. The initial "payment" is in the form of surrender of the sense of worth and self-esteem, but added payment is soon extracted.

Self-atonement, commonly known in psychological literature as "masochism," is one of the most common methods of escaping the pain of guilt, but it is also one of the most destructive. Far more could be said on the subject than is appropriate here. Indeed, whole books have been written on the subject. Karl Menninger's *Man Against Himself*, published originally in 1938, deserves the designation as a classic on the subject. *The Joy of Suffering* by Shirley Panken is of a more recent vintage, having been released in 1973, and will have to be considered as a part of any serious study of masochism.[3]

The problem of trying to discuss intelligently such a large subject in a few pages is somewhat comparable to trying to discuss the history of China in a thousand words or less.

In brief, one of the most common feelings associated with guilt is the feeling that the guilty self ought to have to pay for his failure. After payment by some form of self-inflicted harm, the pain of guilt is at least temporarily relieved. But since we often feel guilty for bringing harm to any person, including ourselves, a fresh guilt is added to the former for which the self must pay again. A most destructive cycle is established; a behavior or attitude produces the painful feeling of guilt; the feeling that the pain of guilt will diminish if the self is made to pay for the failure; a payment is made in the form of some additional failure; but additional guilt now calls for a fresh payment. Round and round, and down and down goes the destructive cycle that I call "the cycle of the damned."

Though the statement seems self-contradicting,

people often try to make payment for their sense of guilt by heaping additional pain of guilt upon the sense of guilt already suffered. A man may say in effect, "If I suffer enough, and if I'm guilty enough, (for my failings) somehow this will compensate. In other words, I don't have to change my behavior any; I just have to feel guilty.[4] Have we not all heard such people comment, "Oh look what I've done. I'm just terrible. I don't know how people put up with me. I'm the worst mother (husband, wife) in the world."[5] He or she literally wallows in his sense of guilt.

It is the behavior that is self-contradictory: This man makes himself pay for feeling guilty by making himself feel more guilty. We are prone to respond to such statements with, "How dumb!" But is it more dumb than saying that men get drunk because they get drunk, or that they lie because they lie? One man may lie to cover his lie while his neighbor, condemning himself for having gotten drunk, to escape the self-loathing feelings he gets drunk again, in a damning cycle.

This process is readily observed as a contributing factor to alcoholism. A man may have originally gotten drunk for any of a million reasons. Afterward, he may feel that anyone who would so totally lose control to a bottle should be punished. He may turn to alcohol for that punishment. He temporarily feels relief, not only from the opiate effect, but his self-inflicted pain relieves the feelings that make up what we call the guilty conscience. When he later feels the pain of guilt for his behavior, and the need for punishment, he knows that alcohol will help provide the needed misery. Round and round, down and down he goes. He has successfully escaped from freedom![6] This same general process is played out in the drama of the lives of millions, with the script changing but little.

Many a misdeed is almost purely a defective way of

adjusting to the demands of the inner judge. The result is a form of suicide. The story is familiar. It could be enacted as a movie or television drama. A man commits a crime. He puts up a fighting defense to ward off the police. When he realizes the futility of the struggle, he meekly surrenders, only to disarm his captors and escape. The plot thickens as the criminal on the run artfully evades the hounding authorities. An anti-climactic shoot-out leaves the villain crumpled in the street. We get a flash of an unknown face with tear-filled eyes as the scene fades. There is a moment to reflect. Did the police really overcome him or had he set up his own execution? Such things have really happened! I have talked with those who survived it!

When we think that perhaps the story has ended, the image begins to clear with a courtroom coming into focus. Our wounded villain is on trial. We hear the brief essentials and the region's renowned "hangin' judge" passes down the death sentence. As the camera flashes back and forth from the face of the criminal to the face of the judge, the viewer becomes aware of a curious similarity between the judge and the prisoner. Are they twins? No. Each is a mysterious projection of the other. We get another fleeting glimpse of the sad unknown face in the crowd.

We get brief views of the prisoner on death row already paying for his crime. On the appointed day of the execution, we watch the prisoner, pale and lean, as he trudges each measured step toward the death chamber. The door swings open and our eyes become glued to the electric chair. Then we notice the figure standing beside it. The judge! The camera again flashes repeatedly from the face of the criminal to the face of the judge. There is no question. They are the same. They will die together! A hand reaches for the switch. We see a brief scan of the faces of the witnesses and the camera stops at one. It is the now-familiar tear-stained face that has seemed always to be somewhere in the background. He speaks. "Stop! I pardon him." It is the Governor! The viewers sit stunned in disbelief. Some at the Governor's pardon; some at the prisoner's response—"Never mind, Governor, let's get on with it." One hundred thousand volts charge the circuit.

Sages, both ancient and modern, have recognized that the guilty man on the run tends to bring about his own destruction. Plato taught that the soul will run eagerly to its judge.[7] The ancient Seneca taught that every guilty person is his own hangman. Hammarskjold wrote: "We carry our nemesis within us."[8] And Gordon Jackson insists, "The unconscious sense of guilt is identical with the need for punishment."[9]

Osborne writes,

Police report that a criminal will often unwittingly leave some obvious clue at the scene of a crime, an unconscious message to the police, saying, "I am the guilty party. Come and get me!" Consciously he desires to escape. Unconsciously he feels a need to be punished. When apprehended he may feel a temporary relief but not a permanent sense of having expiated his guilt.

As long as he is in prison he may have a mixture of conscious hostility toward the authorities and some sense of relief, for he has been arrested, sentenced, and is paying the penalty for his crime. But when released, still feeling unforgiven by God, man, and his inner judicial self, he will often go to great pains to get himself locked up again. Outside prison walls again, his unresolved guilt takes over, and he feels a need to be punished in order to relieve the sense of guilt.[10]

I once counseled a man who tried to bring about his own execution with a policeman's gun. With two bullets in his body, he said, "I felt cleansed and had a sense of peace before I hit the floor." A man will kill the feelings of guilt or the feelings of guilt will kill the man.

The mid-1970s saw two cases make national news as prisoners fought in the courts to get the state to take their lives. Gary Gilmore succeeded and died in Utah before a firing squad on January 17, 1977.

If the pain of guilt is strong enough, a person feels overwhelmed. His "courage to be" is defeated. When William Shakespeare penned the words, "To be, or not to be," his story character, Hamlet, teetered on the brink of self-destruction. He was as many others before and since his time. Without some form of redemption, he could not bear to go on. He faced annihilation.[11] Such a person may consciously, intentionally kill himself. When the personality is already disintegrating, the crumbling may suddenly develop into a personality avalanche ending in suicide.

Though the statement may make little sense to many at first thought, the truth is that a man may kill himself in his efforts to save himself. In death he may see himself as saving himself from the condemning conscience and its torment. He is somewhat like the criminal who may kill himself rather than endure a long prison sentence.

But even more likely, his own inner judge will turn him over to the inner executioner, intending that the death sentence be carried out. It becomes the big payoff one makes against himself when he gets a glimpse of what he has done to himself and others.[12] It seems to be the only solution when his elaborate defense system has failed. He sees no other way of dealing with his guilt. He feels the ultimate disgust. He looks into the mirror of his soul and says, "You make me sick." Such disgust easily turns to rage. His suicide then becomes an act of murder—murder of the self.

Yes, we have looked at some extreme measures of dealing with guilt, but the inner judge often deals in extremes, and suicide must be classified as the most extreme method of coping with the guilty conscience.

Of course, the reasons for suicide are as varied as the people who attempt it, and no person knowledgeable in the field of suicideology would try to suggest guilt as the only motivation for suicide. It is but one among many. No matter what the pace of destruction, by the slow erosive process or by the emotional landslide that produces suicide, guilt works toward the end result of death. The wages of true guilt *is* death. It works toward the death of the personality. Is there no way out? Is there no truly constructive way of dealing with our guilts?

Indeed there is.

nine

GUILT FREE

Of every method chosen for escaping, evading, easing, eliminating, or paying for release from the pain of the guilty conscience, only two or three have been constructive to human personality. None were adequately pro-life. With few exceptions, all have served as a form of distortion, denial, or escape from reality. Others have served as a payment for having admitted guilt. Each coping device or mechanism of adjustment discussed in the foregoing pages generally has added to the personality sickness, each becoming something of an infected bandage applied to an already diseased wound. Each effort to solve the problem has tended to make the problem worse.

Because the sense of guilt grows out of the violation of our own internal legal system, we seem to want to believe that the guilt problem could be settled purely within. But as we have seen time and again within the pages of this study, guilt is more than an inner conflict. Our real guilt has usually included others. We have truly harmed others to some degree. True guilt is, therefore, an interpersonal problem and requires interpersonal efforts at solution. Where then, do we turn for help?

Guilt, probably more than any other influence, has been responsible for the rise of the psychologically oriented professions. The therapist may go under the title of psychologist, pastoral counselor, psychiatrist, psychiatric social worker, or under any number of other similar professional headings. And within their own ranks the different schools of thought could form a list as long as one's arm. And with few exceptions, all the offices are crowded. Anyone who hangs out a shingle will probably get his share. Some who come will find healing. Others will get sicker.

The turn to the therapist in itself may be an expression of the basic problem. It may be a part of the effort to avoid the real issue. It is far easier to face a stranger whom I see occasionally than to face the one I have harmed the most. If I have offended my wife, I cannot resolve the relationship problem alone with a counselor. If I have insulted my wife, or stolen from my employer, or lied about my neighbor, I cannot retreat to a therapist's office for final resolution of my guilt. Yes, I may walk away *feeling* better, but deep within I know that I am truly guilty and have not yet dealt with the people I have offended. The gap between me and those I offended may be only widened by my delay and by *my* feeling better, while the problem in our relationship is yet unattended. The sense of peace growing out of my therapy may assist me to live in a "fool's paradise" while my relationships continue to crumble.

And all too often one's worsened condition will be *because* of his therapist! His sense of guilt may be increased by the therapist's subtle condemnation, or his system of denial may get additional support by hearing that all his damaging behavior is someone else's fault. His "therapeutic advice" may range from, " . . . it's time you stopped feeling guilty,"[1] to, "If you will just repeat that which makes you feel guilty, you will eventually stop feeling guilty." And a therapist's religious comments may range from "God-is-the-answer; Good-bye" to "I won't even listen to your foolish conversation that includes god-talk." And I have to say, and I don't expect many professional therapists to disagree, that as often as not, God is barred from the therapy office.

Having borrowed or brought many truly valuable tools from other therapists, many gospel ministers also have bought the "nontheistic" philosophy for their pastoral counseling. My more than twenty years of pastoral counseling has convinced me that when people have bypassed half a dozen competent therapists to get to the gospel minister, they have diagnosed their plight as having a significant spiritual dimension. Even they expect (and need) their therapist to have some distinctively Christian contribution to make to their healing process.

Not only have many ministers removed God from the therapy setting, they have apparently forgotten the good news that relates guilt to forgiveness. At a national meeting of several hundred ministers, during a period of response to panelists, the subject had turned to "forgiveness." One man rose and inquired, "I thought we were here to discuss guilt. What has all this talk about forgiveness got to do with the subject?"

Pastoral counselors and other therapists, all too often, have joined in on the counselee's efforts to deny, rationalize, or justify. "Seducing your brother was not so bad. After all, your father had raped you only a few weeks earlier. You were only acting out your hostilities against men." Such efforts to justify are pure poison to the human personality.

On the basis of early childhood experience or parental

failures or somebody else's misbehavior, the therapist tries to exonerate the client from fault. Such release from personal responsibility only serves as a poison to his emotional system, or at best, it is as an aspirin for his cancerous attitudes and behavior that are destroying him. In a day when an aspirin to relieve the pain was the only treatment available, such treatment might have been necessary, but in our modern day, such maltreatment is unthinkable.

Why must a therapist offer his justification for a client when God's forgiveness is available? Efforts to justify may be accurate in their evaluations and high in their motive. But they are harmful!

Behind such vain efforts to accept the counselee, there is concealed an attitude of rejection. And it is only thinly veiled and at a lower level of consciousness, the counselee knows it. He knows that the therapist is secretly agreeing, "What you did is so terrible that I can accept you only by offering some excuse for you."

True acceptance agrees but offers grace! "Yes, what you did was bad, in that you degraded yourself and you participated in something that contributed to the tearing down and erosion of something valuable in your brother, but I'm not going to hold that against you." And the Christian therapist can add, "And my experience declares that God has been wanting to forgive you also." *Any response to true guilt that is short of forgiveness and changed behavior is not only inadequate but it often contributes to further demoralization.*

When the therapist is in the role of the priest or minister, an additional problem arises. The struggling penitent may lose confidence and he may lose hope. He may reflect later. "If my minister says *what I did* is not so bad, he doesn't understand." Or, "If *that's* the highest standard of God, he certainly is no deity worthy of my high esteem." But no matter what the immediate response, at a deeper level of consciousness, one knows he is still guilty, no matter what this authority has said.

Consequently, his guilt is still on him, but it lives at a damaging level that will rarely urge him to seek forgiveness. "If there is nothing to forgive, I will simply have to learn to accept this vague uncomfortable feeling (guilt) and live with it. If there isn't anything bad about my behavior, there isn't anything to be forgiven for. I'll just have to go on carrying the load or I'll have to pay for it." Opportunity for forgiveness and true release is therefore closed! And it is often closed by the psychotherapist or by the gospel minister who could and should be an agent of forgiveness and reconciliation! Guilt must be taken seriously. When people have harmed themselves and others, *they are guilty!*

How strange it would seem to hear a medical doctor say to his patient with cancer, "Go to your pastor for all your treatment." Not one pastor in ten thousand has the expertise to perform all the needed help. We want to believe that the odds are not so high when looking for a medical doctor who is adequately equipped to help one deal with the problem of guilt. But guilt is basically a spiritual problem. It is unfair that organized Christianity has put the blame on the psychotherapist for secularizing the problem of sin and guilt, as well as its solution. All too often, the church has abdicated the field. David Belgum reminds us of the popular practice that "if a man commits adultery, embezzles money from his company, or does other immoral acts, the clergyman, as well as the judge, recommends psychotherapy."[2] Though the psychotherapist may certainly help one deal more constructively with false guilt, when adequately understood and meditated, no person on earth has more to meet the needs of the truly guilty than the one who communicates the love of God as revealed in Jesus Christ! And the mediated love of God is quite often needed in the final stage of therapy even in dealing with false guilt.

Remember the law of momentum. When applied to the personality, we called it the "law of mortigression," which says: "A personality in the process of deterioration, tends to continue in the process of deterioration *unless acted upon by an outside force.*" One outside force is needed to stop both the erosive behavior that produces guilt and the reduction of pain of the guilty conscience. That force is *love,* and it is experienced in *forgiveness*.[3]

The force (dynamic) of love seems to be recognized by mankind in every level of civilization. Its presence, or lack of presence, is seen at virtually every facet of every culture. Look at the art, the literature, and the legend. Look at man's law, his music, and his religion. Love, or the lack of love, are the most powerful forces known to man.

Love, experienced in forgiveness, reduces the guilty conscience to only a memory with regret. This kind of love works only for the best interests of the recipient. It holds no grudge and demands no payment. In fact, if one tries to receive it by payment, he does not receive it at all. He must receive it as a free gift. Go out and try to buy love. What you receive is only an empty, meaningless symbol of what love could be.

Every counselor has experience with those who have spent a lifetime trying to get someone to love them. They have tried to barter for love by offering good behavior or loyalty or labor. While love, in reality, may be extended toward the one trying to work or earn it, what he receives is experienced as something less than love. Love will be received freely or it will not be received as love at all.

Love received, then, in a specific form such as forgiveness or mercy is commonly called "grace." It is grace because it is not earned or merited in any way. The grace of forgiveness must come unconditionally, if it is to come as an act of love.

The problem with which we are struggling becomes more complex by the moment. Nothing is simple about accepting love in the form of forgiveness. We may like the idea of someone loving us by having some sort of warm feeling toward us, but we may get uncomfortable when the love comes through clearly enough for us to benefit by it. Love coming in our direction may be delightful, but placing ourselves in the receptive stance requires something of us. That, we may not necessarily like.

Love accepted requires that we be no longer isolated. Love accepted suggests that we are no longer totally independent. We are dependent upon someone outside ourselves to fill a part of our need. We admit we are not totally self-sustaining. Love realized from outside requires that we admit that we are not as totally independent as we want to make ourselves believe.

Of course, we are looking into the face of a conflict. One part of the self wants another person inside its world, while another part of the personality wants to remain alone. We seem to live with the common feelings, "I don't want to need anyone." Even as we see this trait within ourselves we are aware that it is generally recognized that the healthy personality requires community. Personalities must interact in order to remain healthy. Ernest Ligon, a psychologist renowned for his studies in character research, insists that "it has been thoroughly demonstrated that social isolation is almost certain to lead to mental disease, and that social interest is essential to mental health."[4]

We tend to be more like Robinson Crusoe than most

want to admit. Remember that when he was marooned on a desolate island, for the first several years Robinson Crusoe longed for companionship. But the day he first saw Friday's footprint in the sand he panicked. He rushed to secure his fortress and to prepare his weapons for defense. It seemed obvious to him that any person who invaded his private world would want to do him harm. The very thing he had longed for he now feared.

We commonly tell ourselves that we want others to live in our world but all too often we are kidding ourselves. We are afraid of others. We are afraid of their criticism or of their rejection. We tend to build our defenses to fortify our position and to camouflage who we are and where we are. We fear vulnerability. Men often conclude, "If another is close enough to know me, he is close enough to hurt me."

We look at ourselves and our behavior, and deep within we know that our behavior has wounded others. We have rejected others. We have deflated another's ego. We have been false. We have contributed to the state of the world in which we live. We have wasted the fossil fuels by leaving the lights burning in unoccupied rooms. We have helped contribute to the pollution of the air by driving automobiles that pump harmful gasses from the exhaust pipes. And we have helped destroy the life in our streams by failing to adequately finance sewage treatment facilities. People have been hurt by our actions and by our inactions. Though our part may have been small or even indirect, we have made our contributions to the wounds of others.

When we have hurt people, we have become alienated. When others have not cut us off, we have cut ourselves off. We have alienated ourselves. We have turned and fled in terror of being found out. We have hid from others and we have harmed ourselves. Like an

Adam or Eve, we have either tried to hide from God or we have gone even farther and have tried to completely eliminate him by denying he even exists. With such attitudes and behavior, we feel surely that any savage invader to our island is there to harm us, even if only by the hurling of a disapproving glance.

Love often comes as one "islander" reaching out to another "islander"; one isolated soul reaching out to another isolated soul. When Friday was no longer just a footprint in the sand, but was met as another soul struggling for survival, the two were still worlds apart with all but impossible barriers separating them. Our mutual fear and distrust diminishes only as we gain the courage to venture out from concealment, or if we realize that we have been seen in an unguarded moment and were not attacked. Love that accepts us is the love that provides enticement and nurtures courage. As courage grows, we shed more of our protective cover and come out of hiding. But the atmosphere must be secure. As one man said to his wife in the marriage counseling office, "How can I admit that I'm wrong if I know I'm going to be attacked? A man defends himself from getting hurt."

Emotionally, the coming out of hiding is a kind of confession—a step toward health. It is seeing our behavior as degrading and harmful to ourselves or to others, and as such, we admit we have been wrong (guilty).

Confession no longer declares, "Not I." Confession cries, "I'm the one. I have failed. I have helped pollute the air by driving an improperly tuned automobile. I have helped waste the earth's energy resources. I have closed my eyes to those who hunger. I have remained silent or have been secretly pleased as men rot unproductively in prisons. I am not giving adequate time and affection to my growing children. I must confess before I can change to behavior more beneficial to others and to myself. It is I who may need to work to restore what I have damaged."

The failure to recognize the need for restoration may well be the most important single missing factor in modern man's struggle with guilt. But few want to recognize the need. It can be quite expensive. It requires that where possible, and without causing further injury, we restore what we have damaged, whether from a man's purse or from his reputation. Practicing protestant theology has accurately emphasized the need for accepting grace (unmerited favor as expressed in forgiveness) but too often it has overemphasized "grace plus faith (in God) plus nothing." The emphasis on "nothing" too often has neglected the need to restore. While men are often exhorted to make things right with God and the neighbor, the exhortation is left hanging as a vague abstraction. Restoration (making things right) must become concrete.

If I have stolen your purse, a mere confession with apologies and plea for forgiveness is empty if I walk away with your money still in my pocket. Though restoration is one of the most positive attacks against forces of guilt, it is not always that uncomplicated. Restoration requires the conscious intent with effort to do something constructive to lessen the damage accomplished by the original misdeed. The phrase, "lessen the damage" is quite important. And it must remain important, lest in the effort to restore, even more harm may be brought to the person originally harmed.

A story has often been repeated of a woman who had scattered malicious, false stories of a man of her village. In remorse, she turned to a wise man, asking how she could "make right" her terrible misdeed. The wise man sent her out to scatter all the feathers from her pillow throughout her village. When she returned the next day to report the task complete, he sent her back to collect them again. When she returned many days later having regathered only a small number, she wept in despair. "It's impossible."

The old sage responded, "Go now to those who have heard your stories. Correct them all."

"But," cried she, "my evil stories about my neighbors are as the feathers scattered to the four winds—nay, they are worse. Some would be fanned to a greater distance by my flurry of words about the subject. Even dung smells worse when it is stirred."

"You are gaining wisdom, my child," said the wise man. "Many wrongs can never be corrected. When you see the futility of your efforts to fully restore all you have damaged, do not despair. Only then are you prepared to understand any mercy offered by God and others you offended. Accept the forgiveness offered you by God and seek the forgiveness of your neighbor and go in peace."

A step toward lasting sobriety taught by Alcoholics Anonymous requires that one shall "make direct amends to such people wherever possible, except when to do so should injure them or others." Steps taken to compensate for, or neutralize damage done, puts muscle into the act of confession.

The question often arises: "But what of confession as it relates to God?" The Scriptures clearly teach that confession is a step in the process of reconciliation with him. "If we confess our sins, he is faithful and just to forgive our sins, and to cleanse us from all unrighteousness."[5]

Love experienced as forgiveness has a cleansing effect on the personality. One effect of guilt is the accompanying feelings of dirtiness. The Scriptures often speak of people "defiling" themselves, making themselves "impure." The guilty psalmist sought to be cleansed by washing in the loving forgiveness of Jehovah.[6] The Bible often speaks of God as One who cleanses. The Protestant wants to know immediately, "But what of another person's involvement? We don't have to admit our humiliating faults to anybody but God, do we?" Maybe some few don't, but most would do well to involve another human. The New Testament clearly teaches, "Confess your faults to one another, and pray for another, that you may be healed."[7] We Protestants must concede that everything that came out of the Reformation was not necessarily for the best. Even Martin Luther recognized the value of confession. About him, Edgar Jackson writes:

It was to the abuses of the confessional that Luther in part addressed himself in his Ninety-Five Theses. It was not that he did not value confession, but he believed it should be voluntary and shorn of those abuses that made it little more than a monetary transaction. For himself, he says, "I would let no man take confession away from me, since I know what comfort and strength it has given me."[8]

Contrary to popular belief among Protestants, and even many of older Christian tradition, the priest is not in and of himself the only forgiver.

The priest is only the channel through which men gain God's forgiveness. One does not confess to the priest as a person but to God through the priest. The priest is there to help the penitent formulate his sin and to be the visible transmitter of God's grace of forgiveness.[9]

One of the most important functions of the priest, the gospel minister, the psychotherapist, or the friend who hears confession, is to provide a secure atmosphere that communicates, "I will try to love you in spite of your faults." If we are both unattacked and loved (accepted), even as we are, then we are freer to be even more honest with ourselves and with others. It is often necessary that we find acceptance from another before we can ever find ourselves acceptable.

As Robinson Crusoe was unattacked and accepted in spite of his weaknesses and his failures, he then began to show evidences of becoming more whole. One accepting soul appears to have saved him from total personality disintegration. Defoe, as he wove the story, probably had no thought of the near-universal truths of human nature, but the implications of truth are there, none the less.

Anyone who has worked with the severely emotionally troubled has seen one person make the difference. One loving, caring, accepting person, who saw the failures, the indignities, the stains, but who refused to hold the very worst to his charge, made the difference. The guilt feelings vanished![10]

If the care, the concern, the acceptance, the love of one person can make the difference between life and death; if it can motivate one to turn from a pro-death to a pro-life pattern of behavior, might such a force be collected and channeled? This is basically the theory of group psychotherapy. The group, communicating love, entices self-revelation. It encourages the facing of reality. As one unveils himself, the outside force of forgiving, accepting love motivates change—a change in attitude and change in behavior.

One healing community, commissioned with the task of loving, was established nearly two thousand years ago and continues to this day. It was established for the purpose of helping human beings to know the experience of being loved. That healing community of individuals was called the Church and its founder was Jesus of Nazareth, Christ, the Son of God. That body of persons, with Christ as its head, has the potential for being the most powerful force of love on the face of the earth. It can do so only where it accepts its responsibility! The Church was established as a community of love, of forgiveness, of healing. Apart from that function it is in danger of being reduced to little more than another social club. All too often the Church has wanted only to tell of the love of God as revealed in Jesus Christ without trying to be a channel or mediator of that love. It was intended to be both.

But whether the love is from one human personality, from the Church, or directly from God, healing will be completed only to the degree it is accepted. Love has healing potential when it says, "I accept you." But I must accept your acceptance! Healing love, expressed as forgiveness says, "Your misbehavior I do not hold against you. I do not hold to your charge that which you have done or have failed to do. You are pardoned." But to be healed, I must accept the forgiveness! Forgiveness requires a complete transaction: "Please forgive me." "I forgive you." "I accept your forgiveness." Only then can reconciliation be accomplished. Forgiveness, therefore, may be said to remove the barrier between personalities.[11]

Once accepted, experienced, and realized, forgiveness is recreative. It is pro-life in the face of pro-death behavior and attitudes. Love recognizes that men are not always good. Indeed, it says, "Though you are not good, I love you anyway." Men commonly believe they must be "good" if they are to be loved by God. Even a cursory reading of the New Testament reveals that "the message of the Early Church was not that man could be so awfully good, but that he could be so loved in spite of his failure to be good, and that the more he could allow himself to be loved, the more his possibilities for good could be enhanced."[12] The message of the written Word of God, the Bible, repeatedly conveys the idea that in spite of the fact that men repeatedly harm themselves and others, being therefore guilty, God comes as a loving outside force motivating the stopping of destructive behavior, and beginning a pattern of constructive behavior. We are looking at far more than just remorse; a sense of regret for the past. Hope lies in possible change. This change, that the New Testament calls "repentance," is away from a pro-death to a pro-life style. True repentance offers hope for the future.[13]

Therefore, one outcome of the awareness of guilt can be change. Many believe that feelings of guilt cannot possibly have any value when in reality one of the healthiest ways of dealing with a guilty conscience is to change the behavior that is producing it. Whether the pollution is to our streams by industrial waste, to our lungs by tobacco smoke or to our souls by greed, unless we take personal responsibility, we die. Only as we accept personal responsibility may we recognize that we have the ability to repent (change) and live.

While some schools of thought would have us believe that we are so bound by our past that we cannot change, every therapist expects change in attitude if not in behavior. A major tenant of transactional analysis therapy is the importance of "redecision." This personality science places heavy emphasis on the use of the will and the place of decision in the changing on one's circumstances. "Even popular newspaper and magazine articles speak in glowing terms about the rehabilitated prisoner, the recovered alcoholic, and the person who has openly 'turned over a new leaf.' Such persons are in a very real sense 'restored to the community.' "[14] "The psychoanalyst recognizes the value of the sense of guilt that is realistic and constructive, which results in action to change what must be changed."[15] Psychoanalytic theory seems, at times, to suggest that the personality is formed in concrete—unchangeable, but the very practice of analysis recognizes a value in guilt and its urge to change.

The very allusion to change points to a great paradox within psychoanalytic writings. The same extensive writings about how one is absolutely determined by his early experiences, go on to emphasize life-changing results of psychoanalytic therapy. Man is free to change! James Knight reminds his readers:

One should never forget that in spite of Freud's deterministic viewpoint and his great emphasis on the past as the conditioner of the future, he involved himself in the treatment of patients with the intention of liberating them, at least in part, from the bondage of the past. Thus, no matter what might have been his theories, in practice he gave vivid testimony for the existence of freedom in man through capacity to change.[16]

Dr. Karl Menninger, a pioneer in behavioral research, is not particularly kind to his colleagues who would have us believe that we are so bound to our past that we have no freedom to change. On the basis of studies by internists of the Menninger Foundation and their research in biofeedback, Dr. Menninger speaks of conclusive evidence that men have even the ability to take voluntary control of blood pressure and heartbeat irregularities. "Even epilepsy, an electrical storm in the brain, is yielding in some cases to self-regulation of brain-wave patterns through biofeedback training. . . .

To admit the notion of any 'voluntary' control is to acknowledge that such intangibles as idealism and conscience and 'will' do play a determining factor in human behavior."[17] Such awareness is of no recent discovery, unless one thinks of biblical writing as "recent."

Personal revelation, however, may require some reflection before change is affected. After several hours in the counseling process, a counselee reluctantly told of behavior that was resulting in extreme feelings of guilt.

"What on earth am I going to do?"

I responded, "Susan, you have several choices. You can conjure up some justification for your behavior. You can come up with any number of methods of denying to yourself that you are really harming yourself and Tom. You can . . ." and she interrupted.

"Or I can change my way of acting."

"Right! *If* you couple the change with forgiveness."

"You mean forgiveness from Tom."

"Right again. You need to do whatever you can to make things right between the two of you. And you need forgiveness from the person who most loves the one you have harmed."

"Why do I need forgiveness from that person?"

"Because you have wounded that person also. For instance; since I love my children, if you offended one of them, you have offended me also. In a similar, but much greater way, God the Heavenly Father loves the person you injured. God is, therefore, hurt that you have wounded his child. But that's not all. He is further hurt by your injury to at least one other person."

"I was afraid you might try to bring God into this somehow. Are you bringing him into the conversation because you are a minister?"

"No. It's the other way around. One of the reasons I am a minister is because I am convinced that God is already a part of such problems as you have described, and that for the problem to be dealt with adequately, God has to be dealt with as a part of the solution."

"All right. I need to seek God's forgiveness. But somewhere in the conversation I believe you suggested that I needed forgiveness of at least one other person."

"You heard correctly! Since you injured Tom, if you examine the situation carefully, I believe you will see that you injured at least one other person and that person is really quite irritated by your behavior and even now is carrying a grudge against you."

"You don't have to say any more. I'm angry with myself, and I'm disgusted with myself. I have been ever since I admitted to myself that what I had done was wrong." There was a moment of reflection, and then more hesitation, "Chaplain, this sounds crazy to me but, ever since I admitted to myself that what I did to Tom was wrong, somewhere inside of me I keep feeling something that tells us that I ought to have to pay for my mistake. Does that sound sort of silly to you?"

"Not at all. In fact, people do often hurt themselves as a way of reducing the pain of the guilty conscience. I hate to tell you but, on the basis of what you have said to me, your options are quite limited. The stating of your options becomes something of a terrible prophesy. You will either accept forgiveness for your repeated injury to Tom or you will degrade and injure yourself more and more in your vain efforts to make yourself pay. The price you feel needs to be paid in your behalf was paid long ago by Christ upon the cross and he still pays in your behalf as he is wounded while watching you injure Tom and as he still watches you degrade yourself. He loves you and therefore it hurts him to see you participate in behavior that tears you down, making you less of a person than what you otherwise would be."

"Then I need to accept God's forgiveness and I need to go to Tom and see if he will forgive me."

"Right on both issues. But you may have missed an important implication of my comments. You need also to forgive yourself!"

"I've never thought of that. You mean I may need to forgive myself, just as I might forgive someone else?"

"That is precisely what I mean. In your question, you pulled in another important part of the solution to your need for release from your sense of guilt. To find full release from your burden of guilt, you need to accept forgiveness of others. You need to forgive others. And you need to forgive yourself. I'm calling upon you to be as compassionate, merciful, and forgiving of yourself. And at the same time, as a part of your conditioning of yourself for accepting forgiveness, you must forgive others who have done you wrong."

"I've got a lot more to deal with in my efforts to find some peace within myself than I thought."

"I've done far more talking than usual today. In doing so I've tried to give you some idea of some important matters we will need to deal with somewhere along the way. Let's go back to where you were when we got into this conversation. You said earlier that you were beginning to see that your behavior was harming you as much or more than it is harming Tom . . . ."

After an additional three months in the counseling process, Susan had committed her life to God for forgiveness and for day by day leadership, and she and Tom had committed themselves to one another in marriage. We will wish them well, and agree that only the test of time upon their marriage will determine what value or lack of permanent value may have come out of the sessions.

It was the power of love experienced as forgiveness that turned back the tide for Susan. And love is the integrative, outside force that has the power to bind up that which is broken in much of mankind. It is love that has the power to sustain the human character in his day-to-day struggles. Since the love of God is the most certain, the most dependable, the most complete and the strongest love that exists, when accepted, it has the greatest healing power of all love.

When we are talking about healing, we are talking about making whole or putting together more constructively. It is often said to be recreative. The love of God, when permitted to be active in human life is miraculously recreative; so much so that Christianity commonly refers to the miracle of the new birth. The work of love by God has been attested to by people of all ages for nearly two thousand years. Like so many other phenomena, it is not fully understood but it is recognized as a practical experience in the lives of those who practice it. Though electricity is not fully understood, nor defined, none is so foolish that he refuses to tap into its benefits. Yet, when a Being of far greater power for good is mentioned, many would deny his reality. They flee the power of recreative love.

Forgiveness has been symbolized as a key in a lock. David Belgum reminds us that,

The sole purpose of turning a key in a lock is to unlock the door and to enable one to go into the next room, i.e. to pass out of bondage into freedom. It is not enough to be stuck or fixated in a key-turning syndrome. The goal is not forgiveness, but the restored fellowship with God and neighbor and self for which forgiveness paves the way. And fellowship involves the willingness of both parties.[18]

When men recognize that God is so loving that he desires only the best for mankind, in faith they commit themselves to follow his leadership as he provides it through his written Word. He speaks leading principles by way of the Bible and he leads the spirits of men in the day-to-day events by his Holy Spirit who walks with men each step of the way.

He who walks in communion with God may face his true guilts, with no cause to fear—no need to hide—no reason to evade the truth. The guilty man is still acceptable to God. Listen carefully. When the voice of God says, "You're guilty," he also says, "but I still love you." Listen carefully. The voice that says, "You're guilty," may be the voice of God calling to repentance, calling to life, calling to fellowship.

But the call of God as seen in his written Word, the Bible, is never a call to idleness. Jesus Christ's last known recorded words spoken while yet in human flesh were the call to evangelize; to carry the good news; God loves you too![19] God is still calling us to see our error, to accept forgiveness, to changed lives, to improving the world in which we live.

REVIEW

COPING MECHANISMS

I. Offensive Defense (chapter 3)

1. **Repetition**—"If I keep committing the offense often enough, I'll stop feeling so bad about it." p.43
2. **Balancing**—"If I do lots of other 'good' things, I won't feel bad about the 'bad' things I do." p.43
3. **Confession**—"I'll admit my faults and purge myself of them—after all, if I'm willing to admit this fault, I'm not such a bad person after all, am I?" p.44

II. Surrender to Guilt Feelings (chapter 4)

4. **"That's Just the Way I Am"**—"I'm not responsible—look how my parents treated me as a child—I was born under the sign of Capricorn; it was written in the stars I'd be this way. I'm just the way God made me." p.48
5. **Passage of Time**—"It's been a long time since I did it. I hardly ever think about it, much less feel bad about it anymore." p.48
6. **Self-Recrimination**—"I'm just an awful, terrible person!" ("I hope someone will say; 'Come now, you're not so bad!' Nobody's saying anything. Maybe I'd better say it again, louder.") "**I'm such a terrible, terrible person!**" p.49
7. **Everybody's Doing It**—"Everybody rips off the company. I don't do anything worse than the other fellows." p.49

III. Escape from Guilt Feelings (chapter 5)

8. **Suppression**—"I feel really bad about it, but if I can just keep from thinking about it, I'll be all right—I can live with it." (Similar to trying to hold tennis balls on the bottom of a swimming pool.) p.53
9. **Repression**—"I've got to forget this terrible thing! I won't ever remember it again!" (The memories of details go away but the troublesome feelings remain, like rotting material on the bottom of the swimming pool that keeps polluting the pool every time something stirs it up.) p.54
10. **Knowledge**—"Wow! I didn't know everybody thought things like that. Why, I'm no more guilty than others who have such thoughts." p.56
11. **Distraction**—"If I keep busy, I won't hear my conscience nagging me." (Methods used: sleep, sex, committing crimes for excitement, mental busy-work, working and playing hard.) p.57
12. **Isolation**—"I'll do it, but I just won't think about what I'm doing." "I'll emotionally detach myself from the experience so totally, I will scarcely realize I participated in it." p.60
13. **Masking**—"You may call me a common thief, but really, I'm highly skilled in what I do. I'm a very good safe cracker." "You may call me immoral if you want, but I know a lot of men who think of me as the best strip-tease in the country." p.61
14. **Fantasy**—"Life is so grim—I hurt so bad inside—I just like to dream of myself being in some pleasant place a million miles from here." p.64
15. **Opiates**—"As long as I stay on these pills (drugs, alcohol), I don't feel too bad about what happened." p.64
16. **Insanity**—"I can't face life the way it is anymore." "I'll either kill myself or go crazy!" "I'm not a sinner—don't you realize I'm the only good person in the universe. I'm God!" p.65

IV. Evasion of Guilt Feelings (chapter 6)

17. **Sublimation**—"My urges to have an affair with my secretary make me feel miserable. I'll redirect my energies toward being extra nice to my wife." p.68
18. **Overreaction**—(Reaction formation) "I don't know how anyone could drink that terrible alcohol. I think we should start a campaign to close all these filthy bars in the city." (Loud protests cover a secret desire to partake of the evil, as a man trying to be a Casanova with women to cover up his hidden homosexual desires.) p.69

19. **Denial of Standards**—"All rules are only relative. It might be wrong somewhere else, but I don't consider it wrong in this situation or culture." p.70
20. **Willy Lomanism**—(Fixation) "I usually try to be what others expect me to be. Right and wrong is what others say it is—I never thought much about it myself." p.70
21. **Regression**—"When I was young, I never worried about all these decisions of what's right and wrong. I feel so bad—I'll take myself back to emotionally being a child again." p.72
22. **Denial**—"There was nothing wrong in what I did. He should have known that I get upset easily." "There's no law that says a man can't defend himself." p.73
23. **Ignorance**—"I didn't know my tires were worn slick, so it's not my fault I couldn't stop." "How am I to be responsible for laws I don't know?" p.75
24. **Perfectionism**—"Forget about the disgraceful creature you really are; this is how you **should** be, and most important, how you should **appear** to be." p.75
25. **Rigid Rightness**—"Of course, I said the Pittsburgh Steelers would win, but that was before Terry Bradshaw got hurt. In principle, they did win." "I said it would snow here; well, it did snow right over in the next county." p.76
26. **Defensive Aggression**—"We've taken the wrong road and now we're lost. Honestly, can't you watch where we're going? Don't I have enough to do to drive this car? The least you could do is to watch the road signs. You have all the maps right there!" (Angry with himself for taking the wrong turn, he blames his wife for the mistake.) p.76
27. **Hate the Harmed**—"I know my wife is badly hurt because I betrayed her, but let her hurt—she deserves to hurt." (Unable to make restitution, the guilty husband derogates his wife to lessen his wrong.) p.77
28. **Scapegoating**—(Projection) "He led me on. I didn't want to do it. He said I was 'chicken' if I didn't do it. It's his fault." p.78
29. **Substitution**—"I've given her diamonds, furs, expensive clothes, cars—I don't know why she isn't happy. Just because I don't like to sit around the house with her all the time, she gets upset." p.83
30. **Undoing**—(Negative magic) "If I go through the ritual of baptism or repeat certain phrases again and again, my misdeed will (magically) not have happened. I'm sorry, I'm sorry, I'm sorry . . . ." p.84
31. **Displacement**—"Everybody embezzles from his company sometime. Of course, I cheat on my income tax—but cheating the paperboy out of his fifty cents—now that

would really be low down." (Disproportionate guilt toward minor offense to mitigate big offense.) p.84

32. **Rationalization**—"I had to take the money. I couldn't possibly earn enough money to make my wife happy on what this tightwad company pays me." p.85
33. **Justification**—(a form of Rationalization) "Of course I stole from him. You should see the way he cheats his customers by charging the wrong prices for goods." "My sales down? Of course, who could sell a product that doesn't work half the time?" p.86
34. **Identification**—"Cigarette smoking can't possibly be wrong. Charles Spurgeon smoked. C. S. Lewis smoked a pipe." "French Christians don't see anything wrong with drinking wine." p.87
35. **Chance**—"A lot of other people were there when his boat turned over. Any one of them could have jumped in to try to save him. Many of them were just as close to him as I was. It's possible he would have died even if I had gone after him." p.88
36. **Dilution**—(similar to Chance) "A lot of other people heard her scream, too. Why single me out? I'm no more responsible than the other people in the building." "Who killed President Kennedy? We all did. We all allowed such unrest to exist in our society that would produce a Lee Harvey Oswald. We are all guilty" (Therefore, none of us is very much.) p.89
37. **Approval**—"Pastor, tell me now. You don't think I'm a rotten person on my way to hell just because I drink a beer every now and then, do you?" "Jesus drank, didn't he?" "I know it seems unfair, but I really didn't do anything illegal, now, did I?" p.89
38. ***Forgiveness***—"Yes, I have failed to be the person I ought to be. I accept your forgiveness, the forgiveness of God, and I forgive myself." (Chapter 9)
39. ***Repentance***—(coupled with forgiveness) " . . . and with God's help, accepting his leadership of my life, I am changing my attitude and behaviors." (Chapter 9)
40. ***New Birth***—(coupled with forgiveness and repentance) "My God—by some miracle I cannot fully understand, now that I am trusting you, you have cleansed me from my wrong and have made a new person of me." (Chapter 9)

NOTES

CHAPTER ONE

1. Albert Ellis, *Reason and Emotion in Psychotherapy* (New York: Lyle Stuart, 1962), pp. 133, 137.
2. Reported by B. David Edens, "Youngsters Are Frightened," *Baptist and Reflector,* News Journal of the Tennessee Baptist Convention, Vol. 145 No. 6, Feb. 7, 1979, p. 12.
3. David Viscott, *Feel Free* (New York: Dell, 1974), Cover.
4. Karl Menninger, *Whatever Became of Sin?* (New York: Hawthorn Books, 1973), p. 19.
5. Nicolas Berdyaev, *The Destiny of Man* (New York: Harper & Row, 1960), p. 187.
6. Thomas A. Harris, *I'm O.K., You're O.K.* (New York: Harper & Row, 1967).
7. *Makers of the Modern Theological Mind* (Waco, Tex.: Word).
8. Cecil Osborne, *The Art of Understanding Yourself* (Grand Rapids: Zondervan, 1967), p. 96.
9. Nathaniel Branden, *The Psychology of Self-Esteem* (Los Angeles: Nash Publishing, 1969), p. 160.
10. George Washington quoted by Lawrence J. Peter, *The Peter Prescription* (New York: Bantam Books, 1972), p. 122.
11. John Drakeford, *Integrity Therapy* (Nashville: Broadman Press, 1967), p. 42.
12. David Belgum, ed., *Religion and Medicine* (Ames: Iowa State University Press, 1967), p. 221.

13. Paul Tournier, tr. by Arthur W. Heathcote, *Guilt & Grace* (New York: Harper & Bros., 1962), p. 65.
14. Menninger, *Whatever Became of Sin?*, p. 19.
15. Erich Fromm, *The Heart of Man* (New York: Harper & Row, 1964), p. 47.
16. Meyer Friedman and Ray H. Rosenman, *Type A Behavior and Your Heart* (New York: Alfred A. Knopf, 1974), pp. 63-67; 172-179.
17. Friedman and Rosenman, *Type A Behavior*, p. 172.

CHAPTER TWO

1. Fromm, *The Heart of Man*, p. 47.
2. *The Confessions of Saint Augustine*, tr. by E. B. Pusey (Mount Vernon: Peter Pauper Press, "n.d."), p. 27
3. Fromm, *The Heart of Man*, p. 129.
4. C. S. Lewis, *Mere Christianity* (New York: Macmillan Paperbacks, 1960), p. 19.
5. Ernest M. Ligon, *The Psychology of Christian Personality* (Schenectady: Character Research Press, 1975), p. 14.
6. Karen Horney, *Neurosis and Human Growth* (New York: W. W. Norton, 1950), p. 180.
7. Ellis, *Reason and Emotion in Psychotherapy*, p. 145.
8. George W. Kisker, *The Disorganized Personality* (New York: McGraw-Hill, 1964), p. 142.

CHAPTER THREE

1. Anton S. LaVey, *The Satanic Bible* (New York: Avon Books, 1969), p. 53.
2. Herbert A. Carroll, *Mental Hygiene* (Englewood Cliffs: Prentice-Hall, 1956), p. 53.
3. Caryll Houselander, *Guilt* (New York: Gordian Press, 1971), p. 53.
4. Houselander, *Guilt*, p. 30.
5. William E. Hulme, *Pastoral Care Come of Age* (Nashville: Abingdon Press, 1970), p. 70.

CHAPTER FOUR

1. Bruce Narramore and Bill Counts, *Guilt and Freedom* (Santa Ana, Calif.: Vision House, 1974), p. 31.
2. Karen Horney, *The Neurotic Personality of Our Time* (New York: W. W. Norton, 1937), p. 242.
3. Menninger, *Whatever Became of Sin?*, p. 158.

4. Leslie Weatherhead, *Psychology, Religion and Healing* (New York: Abingdon-Cokesbury Press, 1952), p. 324.
5. Peter, *The Peter Prescription,* p. 228.

CHAPTER FIVE

1. Herbert A. Carroll, *Mental Hygiene* (Englewood Cliffs: Prentice-Hall, 1956), p. 204.
2. This intimate detail has been read and approved for inclusion by the person who experienced it.
3. Karen Horney, *Neurosis and Human Growth,* p. 185.
4. Daniel R. Miller and Guy E. Swanson, *Inner Conflict and Defense* (New York: Schocken Books, 1966), p. 185.
5. Francis P. LeBuffe, *The Hound of Heaven, An Interpretation* (New York: Macmillan, 1958), p. 29.
6. Wayne Oates, *Confessions of a Workaholic* (Nashville: Abingdon, 1971), p. 5.
7. Theodore I. Rubin, *Compassion & Self Hate* (New York: Ballantine Books, 1975), p. 136.
8. Leland E. Hinsie and Robert Jean Campbell, *Psychiatric Dictionary* 4th ed. (New York: Oxford University Press, 1970), p. 414. Quoting Sigmund Freud, *Inhibitions, Symptoms and Anxiety,* 1936.
9. James C. Coleman, *Abnormal Psychology and Modern Life* (Glenview, Ill.: Scott, Foresman, 1964), p. 54.
10. Houselander, *Guilt,* pp. 30-32.
11. Gen. 3:7.
12. Luke 5:8, New American Standard Bible.
13. David Belgum, *Guilt: Where Religion and Psychology Meet* (Minneapolis: Augsburg Publishing House, 1963), p. 7.
14. Norman Cameron, *Personality Development and Psychopathology, A Dynamic Approach* (Boston: Houghton Mifflin, 1963), p. 459f.
15. Howard Clinebell, *Understanding and Counseling the Alcoholic Through Religion and Psychology* (New York: Abingdon Press, 1956), p. 163.
16. David Belgum, "Patient or Penitent" in *Religion and Medicine,* ed. David Belgum (Ames: Iowa State University Press, 1976), p.212.
17. Milton Rokeach, *The Three Christs of Ypsilanti* (New York: Alfred A. Knopf, 1964), p. 134.
18. Ernest E. Bruder, *Ministering to Deeply Troubled People* (Englewood Cliffs: Prentice-Hall, 1963), p. 33.

CHAPTER SIX

1. Cameron, *Personality Development and Psychopathology,* p. 244.
2. Coleman, *Abnormal Psychology of Life,* p. 106.
3. Horney, *Neurosis and Human Growth,* p. 78.
4. Willy Loman was the leading character in the play by Arthur Miller, *Death of a Salesman* (New York: The Viking Press, 1958).
5. Dennis Geaney, *Living with Your Conscience* (Chicago: Thomas Moore Press, 1973), p. 63.
6. Kisker, *The Disorganized Personality,* p. 154.
7. Houselander, *Guilt,* p. 7.
8. Hobart Mowerer, ed., *Morality and Mental Health* (Chicago: Rand McNally, 1967), p. 232.
9. Carol Murphy, "Conscience and Psychotherapy," *Journal of Pastoral Care* (No. 2, 1962), pp. 81-84.
10. Horney, *Neurosis,* p. 64.
11. Horney, *Neurosis,* p. 72.
12. Horney, *The Neurotic Personality,* p. 242f.
13. Paul Tournier, tr. by Arthur W. Heathcote, et al, *Guilt and Grace,* p. 14.
14. John Drakeford, *Integrity Therapy,* p. 37.
15. Abraham Schwartz Ross, "Modes of Guilt Reduction," University of Minnesota, 1965. Order No. 65-15, 217. Abstracted in *Social Psychology,* p. 4855, year unknown.
16. Houselander, *Guilt,* p. 8.
17. Horney, *Neurosis,* p. 64.
18. Matthew 7:3-5; NASB.
19. Charles A. Knight, *For the Love of Money* (Philadelphia: J. B. Lippincott, 1968), p. 68.
20. Horney, *Neurosis,* p. 231.
21. Horney, *The Neurotic Personality,* p. 246.
22. Horney, *Neurosis,* p. 231.
23. David Belgum, "Patient or Penitent," *Religion and Medicine,* p. 211.
24. Coleman, *Abnormal Psychology,* p. 221.
25. Menninger, *Whatever Became of Sin?,* p. 181.
26. Sigmund Freud, *The Problem of Anxiety* (New York: W. W. Norton, 1936), p. 53f.
27. Edward V. Stein, *Guilt: Theory and Therapy* (Philadelphia: Westminster Press, 1968), p. 128.

28. Sidney Jordan, *Personal Adjustments: An Approach Through the Study of Healthy Personality* (New York: Macmillan, 1963), p. 260.
29. Kisker, *The Disorganized Personality*, p. 120.
30. Hensie and Campbell, *Psychiatric Dictionary*, Fourth Ed. p. 645.
31. Jordan, *Personal Adjustment*, pp. 261f.
32. Osborne, *The Art of Understanding Yourself*, p. 87.
33. Osborne, *The Art of Understanding Yourself*, p. 95.
34. Menninger, *Whatever Became of Sin?*, p. 95.
35. Menninger, *Whatever Became of Sin?*, p. 92.

CHAPTER SEVEN

1. Harris, *I'm O.K.–You're O.K.*

CHAPTER EIGHT

1. Branden, *The Psychology of Self-Esteem*, p. 152.
2. *The Confessions of Saint Augustine*, tr. by E. Pusey, p. 36.
3. Shirley Panken, *The Joy of Suffering* (New York: Jason Aaronson, 1973).
4. Earl A. Loomis, *The Self in Pilgrimage* (New York: Harper & Row, 1950), p. 90.
5. James D. Mallory, Jr., *The Kink and I* (Wheaton, Ill.: Victor Books, SP. Publications, 1973), p. 22. Parentheses mine.
6. cf. Erich Fromm, *Escape from Freedom* (New York: Holt, Rinehart, and Winston, 1941).
7. Osborne, *The Art of Understanding Yourself*, p. 99.
8. Dag Hammarskjöld, *Markings*, trans. by Leif Sjöberg and W. H. Auden, Foreword by W. H. Auden (New York: Alfred A. Knopf, 1964), p. 9.
9. Gordon E. Jackson, "The Problem of Guilt" in *Religion and Medicine*, ed. David Belgum (Ames, Iowa: State University Press, 1967), p. 218.
10. Osborne, *The Art of Understanding*, p. 100.
11. Loomis, *The Self*, p. 103, Claudia Naranjo, "I and Thou, Here and Now: Contributions of Gestalt Therapy" in *Gestalt Therapy Primer*, ed. F. Douglas Stephenson (New York: Jason Aronson, 1978), p. 42.
12. For a thorough discussion of man's judgment, condemnation, and execution of himself, see *Guilt and Forgiveness*, William G. Justice (Grand Rapids: Baker, 1980).

CHAPTER NINE

1. Viscott, *Feel Free,* p. 156.
2. David Belgum, *Guilt: Where Religion and Psychology Meet,* p. 63.
3. Earl A. Loomis, *The Self in Pilgrimage* (New York: Harper & Bros., 1960), p. 103, and Richard A. Kalish, *The Psychology of Human Behavior,* 2nd ed. (Belmont, Calif.: Brooks/Cole Pub., 1970), p. 386.
4. Ligon, *The Psychology of Christian Personality,* p. 25.
5. 1 John 1:9.
6. Psalm 51, also cf. Paul Ricouer, *The Symbolism of Evil,* tr. by Emerson Buchanan (New York: Harper and Row, 1967), pp. 25, 33.
7. James 1:16.
8. Edgar N. Jackson, *A Psychology for Preaching* (New York: Hawthorn Books Inc., W. Clement Stone Pub., 1961), p. 124f.
9. H. R. A. Princess Illeana of Romania, *The Spirit of the Eastern Orthodox Church,* Advent Paper Series (Cincinnati: Forward Movement Publications, (n.d.), p. 16.
10. Horney, *The Neurotic Personality of Our Time,* p. 236.
11. Vincent Taylor, *Forgiveness and Reconciliation* (London: Macmillan, 1960), p. 19.
12. Loomis, *The Self,* p. 69.
13. Paul E. Johnson, *Psychology of Religion* (New York: Abingdon, 1945), p. 218f.
14. Belgum, *Guilt: Where Religion and Psychology Meet,* p. 121.
15. William Graham Cole, *Sex in Christianity and Psychoanalysis* (New York: Oxford University Press, 1955), p. 321.
16. James A. Knight, *Conscience and Guilt* (New York: Appleton-Century-Crofts, 1969), p. 25.
17. Menninger, *Whatever Became of Sin?,* p. 78.
18. Belgum, *Guilt: Where Religion and Psychology Meet,* p. 25.
19. Matt. 28:19, 20.

INDEX